THE PIETY OF JEREMY TAYLOR

THE PIETY OF
JEREMY TAYLOR

BY

H. TREVOR HUGHES

LONDON
MACMILLAN & CO LTD
NEW YORK · ST MARTIN'S PRESS
1960

MACMILLAN AND COMPANY LIMITED
London Bombay Calcutta Madras Melbourne

THE MACMILLAN COMPANY OF CANADA LIMITED
Toronto

ST MARTIN'S PRESS INC
New York

PRINTED IN GREAT BRITAIN

To
JEREMY

CONTENTS

FOREWORD

THE author may be forgiven if he uses the first paragraph to
explain how a Methodist minister comes to be writing about
Jeremy Taylor. During my schooldays at the Perse I could
not fail to notice in the assembly hall a large honours board
on which were inscribed the names of old boys who had
obtained Fellowships. There I first came across the name of
Jeremy Taylor, and I was intrigued to hear that he was one
of the most distinguished sons of the Perse; at that time
athletic prowess seemed more important than either
academic distinction or spiritual achievement. Later, I learnt
of his influence on John Wesley, and the combination of
school and church association increased my interest. This
deepened in the years following, and particularly during the
War when Taylor's *Holy Living and Holy Dying* was one of
the few books that I took with me on service overseas. If
there are any misunderstandings or misinterpretations owing
to the fact that the writer is not a member of the Church of
England, he craves the indulgence of those who are.

Until recent years comparatively little had been written
about Taylor in this century. Since the War we have had
books on Taylor's life and writings by Canon Stranks and
Mr Ross Williamson, and an approach to his teaching on
moral theology from Dr H. R. McAdoo and the Rev.
Professor Thomas Wood. The present writer is indebted to
all these authors as well as to those who have written about
Taylor in former days. This volume seeks to deal with
Taylor's piety and to set it in the context of his churchmanship. It does not claim to be a highly original piece of writing
but rather a supplement to what has already been discovered.
Much as I should have liked to increase the number of
quotations from Taylor's writings, succinctness is not one of

his strong points and considerations of space have been severely limiting in this respect.

Piety is a word which has suffered with the passing years. It is used in this work to include all that Taylor has to teach us about how the Christian is to live in relationship with God and his fellows and in the development of his own personality. It is unnecessary to emphasize the need for learning from the masters of Christian piety. However much we may welcome a revived interest in evangelism, new converts and those who grow up inside the Church need guidance and help in the development of Christian character. Again, the ethical implications of Christianity provide problems for the man who seeks to be consistent in his witness. Without sound principles and wise guidance, conscience may be equated with common-sense and the inspiration of the Spirit with intuition or even inclination. It may be of value, whatever criticisms we have of other ages, to look at the principles and practical out-workings of piety in one who was seriously seeking to aid his contemporaries at a time when the casuistry of the Roman Church had fallen into disrepute. Though methods may change, pastoral theology is still of primary importance.

We live at a time when there is a good deal of discussion about the reunion of the Churches. There is, of course, much work to be done in seeking to understand each other's theology and ecclesiastical polity. We ought at the same time to learn more of one another's piety. In one sense we do this already, for the hymns we sing come from the separate Communions of Christ's Church. There is room for further development, in seeking to discover how those in Churches other than our own have tried to foster Christian spirituality in themselves and in those wishing to grow in grace. The agreements of the saints are greater than their divergencies. Unless, alongside our discussions, we can learn from them something of Christian holiness, we may achieve amalgamation but not reunion.

A work of this kind is bound to owe much to the suggestions and kindly criticisms of others. I should like to put on record

the particular debt I owe for help at various stages to Dr
S. G. Dimond, Dr R. Newton Flew, Professor Gordon Rupp
and Professor Thomas Wood. I alone, of course, am responsible for this expression of the piety of Jeremy Taylor.

I owe a special debt of gratitude to my wife for her
encouragement and forbearance in all that the writing of
this book has entailed. I should like to express my thanks
also to my secretary, Miss W. J. Holmes, B.A., for untiring
zeal in helping to prepare the manuscript for publication.

H. TREVOR HUGHES

Westminster College
Oxford

References to Jeremy Taylor's Works are all taken
from the Heber-Eden edition London (1861-5).

Chapter One

BIOGRAPHICAL SKETCH

◆◇◆

The Reformation had many contributory causes but none more important than the upsurge of nationalism in politics and individualism in religion. The desire for freedom from foreign domination combined with a religious awakening which found its earliest stirrings in the activities of Wyclif and his spiritual sons. In the years following Henry's secession the pendulum swung now towards and now away from Rome. The Elizabethan Settlement, while establishing Protestantism, did not at once produce either a developed theology or polity; within the Church men sought publicly and privately, by propaganda or intrigue, to bring both sovereign and country within the sphere of influence of Geneva or Rome.

Such was the position when James came from Scotland to the English throne. 'Scratch a Scot and you will find a theologian' was well illustrated in him, but, as a result of controversy with his Presbyterian subjects, he was an embittered theologian. In the Millenary Petition and the Hampton Court Conference which followed it, he saw again the spirit which he had so mistrusted and disliked in Scotland. On the other hand, the plots of the Papists made a tolerance more congenial to his outlook quite impossible. Politics and religion were so interwoven that generally speaking it was those who would reform the Church who opposed the king. As has been said: 'Unhappily Elizabeth was succeeded by the house of Stuart, who were one and all of them weak despots. The consequence was that dissent identified itself

I

with the national protest against misgovernment.'[1] Religious and political convictions taken separately, as history has demonstrated, provide a powerful dynamic; combined as they were in the reigns of the Stuarts they brought about the melancholy events associated with the seventeenth century.

It was in the time of Charles I that the crisis came. It is not easy to write objectively of either Charles or Laud his archbishop; adulation or abuse have been heaped upon them according to the outlook of their chroniclers. Whatever the virtues of Charles (and he had many) it cannot be denied that he had a flair for misjudging the temper of Parliament and people. Laud unfortunately linked the cause of the Church with that of the king. Though neither was unspiritual, both were intolerant of Puritan spirituality; the rigid enforcement of forms of service was carried out with the best of intentions but it was done at a time when wooing would have been more appropriate than wounding. They adopted a laxer attitude to the sabbath when men of influence were taking a stricter view. The glorification of bishops and an Erastian conception of kingship were ill-suited to the temper of the times. Charles, like Rehoboam of old, was ill-advised; the results were as disastrous for him and his party as for Solomon's son.

That Charles and Laud had no monopoly of intolerance was demonstrated by the Presbyterians in their turn. Some Independents counselled moderation but these sporadic attempts were abortive. Even the advent of the Restoration, with its promise of toleration, did not finally settle the question of religious liberty, for fear of anarchy from within and domination from without delayed the possibility of men living together with forbearance. Peace when it came was coloured by men's memories of civil war and persecution of the people by the people, though ostensibly for the people. Through the stormy days of this century Jeremy Taylor was to pass his life.

[1] C. Bigg, *Wayside Sketches in Ecclesiastical History*, p. 197.

Jeremy was the fourth of six children born to Nathanial and Mary Taylor. Nathaniel, like his father before him, was a churchwarden of Holy Trinity Church, Cambridge. It is said that he carried on his business as a barber just opposite the church. The name of Jeremy Taylor appears in the Parish Register as being baptized on August 15th, 1613; the date of his birth is unknown. He was a pupil of Thomas Lovering first at King's College School and later at the Perse to which Lovering went as headmaster when it was opened in 1619. Taylor was admitted to Gonville and Caius College as a sizar on August 18th, 1626. The admission book says that he was in his fifteenth year. The discrepancy of two years may be due to a desire on the part of Taylor's parents not to risk rejection on the grounds of age, though there were others who had begun their university courses as early as thirteen. If the mistake was due to carelessness on Taylor's part, he would not be the first nor the last student to fail in this respect.

Taylor not only owed his early education to the Perse School; he was indebted to its founder, Stephen Perse, for both a bursary and Fellowship at Gonville and Caius. The former he held from 1628 and relinquished on receiving a junior Fellowship in 1633. This was the year in which he took his M.A. and the probable year of his ordination. When he became a Fellow he was able in part to repay the debt he owed to his benefactor by tutoring his son Martin who came to him with others; one of these was Edward Langsdale, the brother of Taylor's future wife. In 1634 Taylor was appointed *praelector rhetoricus*.

Rust, later Bishop of Dromore, in the sermon that he preached at Taylor's funeral, said that he was a man long before he was of age. Though we know so little about how Taylor achieved his mental and moral stature, the fact that he did so is illustrated by the use he made of an opportunity to deputise for his friend Thomas Risden who was an appointed lecturer at St Paul's. Because of Risden's illness Taylor went as substitute and, according to Rust, 'preached to the admiration and astonishment of his auditory; and by his florid and youthful beauty, and sweet and pleasant air, and sublime and raised discourses, he made his hearers take him for some young angel, newly descended from glory.'[1] We do not know how often Taylor preached again, but the news of his eloquence and sincerity reached Laud who sent for him. The Archbishop seemed satisfied with what he saw and heard; he said that Taylor's only fault was that he was too young. Taylor replied by asking pardon for the fault and promised that 'if he lived he would mend it'.

The next two years of Taylor's life are obscure but in November 1635, after some opposition at Oxford to Laud's suggestion, he was admitted to a probationary Fellowship at All Souls, and became an actual and perpetual Fellow on January 14th, 1636. While at Oxford he increased his knowledge of the Fathers and the ancient classical writers and learnt something of casuistry. He came into close contact with two influential men. One was Francis à St Clara, a Franciscan, who did his best to win Taylor over to Rome. There were even rumours, which Taylor had to repudiate, that he had been successful. Of more influence probably was his friendship with Chillingworth, Laud's godson, whom the prelate had reclaimed from the fold of Rome. Chillingworth loved argument but apparently met his match in Taylor. He declares in a letter that Taylor slights the arguments of his opponents.[2] This is, of course, a common complaint of debaters and no doubt sometimes a just one.

In March 1638, Taylor became Rector of Uppingham. Soon after this he was, on Laud's nomination, appointed Chaplain to the King, and in this year he married Phoebe Langsdale. On November 5th he was in Oxford to preach the annual Gunpowder Treason sermon. It is the first of his surviving writings. The dedication to Laud reveals that Taylor had been appointed as one of his chaplains. Though the sermon is not remarkable either for its substance or style,

---

[1] Taylor, *Works*, I, p. cccxxii.
[2] Des Maiseaux, *Life of Chillingworth*, p. 50.

it is certainly not the product of one who was flirting with Rome. Indeed while at Uppingham he was consulted by a Mrs Turner, wife of the incumbent of Little Dalby, who was under Roman influence. Taylor was not successful apparently in persuading her to remain within the Church of England. She reported that she noticed in Taylor's study a little altar with a crucifix upon it. So, though not a Roman, there would be evidence to support the contention of Barlow that the Puritans regarded Taylor as an extreme High Churchman. This incident suggests that already Taylor had some reputation as a spiritual guide outside his own parish.

Though he succeeded a man who had left the running of the parish to his curate, Taylor was no absentee pastor himself. He was of the Laudian school, and it is therefore not surprising to discover that he took care about the provision of ornaments and vestments. In the Uppingham Parish Register it is stated that on May 10th, 1639, a chalice, two patens, two pewter flaggons, one diaper napkin, one Bible, one Book of Common Prayer, one Altar cloth of green silk damask, two Altar cloths of diaper, two cushions, one tippit, one surplice and two black hoods were dedicated by the Bishop of Peterborough. From the same source we learn that on March 21st, 1638, the Bishop granted a licence for the erection of an organ and recommended that £12 a year should be paid to the organist.

The work at Uppingham had taken Taylor from the academic atmosphere in which he had steeped himself for twelve years to the practical difficulties of ordinary people. Here he met with the cycle of birth, life and death, and experienced in his own home something of the joy and poignancy of a family's hopes, fears and disappointments. The death of his little son William in May 1642, recorded in the Parish Register is witness enough, though we know so little of his life at Uppingham. Domestic sorrow coincided with national trouble. The impeachment of Laud, the decision of Parliament to eject 'all scandalous ministers', the

B

setting up of the royal standard at Nottingham were all symptoms of the gathering storm.

Taylor left Uppingham in the summer of 1642, taking with him the manuscript of *Episcopacy Asserted* and joined the king at Nottingham as one of his chaplains. Charles must have read the book and approved, for he granted Taylor an Oxford D.D. by royal mandate. In 1643 Taylor was appointed to the living at Overstone in Northamptonshire but since the Registers of the parish are no longer in existence we have no knowledge of his life there. He may never have been able to take up his incumbency; the state of turmoil in the country would account for the obscurity surrounding his movements at this time.

When we next hear of Taylor it is as a prisoner captured in the fighting at Cardigan Castle in January 1645.[1] How he got there is a mystery. All Taylor's biographers have exercised their ingenuity to interpret the opening words of *The Liberty of Prophesying* which give a clue to the events. 'In this great storm which hath dashed the vessel of the church all in pieces, I have been cast upon the coast of Wales, and in a little boat thought to have enjoyed that rest and quietness which in England in a greater I could not hope for. Here I cast anchor, and thinking to ride safely, the storm followed me with so impetuous violence, that it broke a cable, and I lost my anchor; and here again I was exposed to the mercy of the sea, and the gentleness of an element which could neither distinguish things nor persons. And but that He who stilleth the raging of the sea, and the noise of His waves and the madness of His people, had provided a plank for me, I had been lost to all the opportunities of content or study. But I know not whether I have been more preserved by the courtesies of my friends, or the gentleness and mercies of a noble enemy.'[2]

Though we cannot speak with certainty, it may be that Taylor left the king at Oxford and joined with two acquaintances, William Wyatt and William Nicholson (both former

---

[1] Whitelocke, *Memoirs*, p. 130.   [2] *Works*, V, p. 340.

Oxford men), in starting a school at Newton Hall close to Golden Grove. No sooner had the work begun than the war reached Wales. Taylor had already had experience as an army chaplain and would therefore be a most suitable person to serve again. He was captured but released through the influence of Lord Carbery and others and because of the generosity of Colonel Laugharne, his captor. He returned to his school and shortly after was appointed as domestic chaplain to Lord Carbery at Golden Grove. The writer agrees with Canon Stranks who identifies Laugharne as the noble enemy as against Gosse and Mr Ross Williamson who have assigned that role to Carbery. Is it likely that Taylor would refer to one who together with his wife had shown him great kindness as an enemy, especially when the book with its dedication might fall into his hands while Taylor was his guest? An error of taste and tact of that sort can hardly be laid at Taylor's door. His various biographers have agreements and divergencies about the cause of Taylor's journey to Wales; they interpret differently the passage quoted from the dedication but all are agreed that he found at Golden Grove the peace he had been seeking.

It was in this haven that Taylor's literary career really began. Apart from the *New and Easy Institution of Grammar* (1647) of which Wyatt wrote the major part, Taylor's works at this period were concerned with debatable matters of the faith. In 1646 he published *A Discourse Concerning Prayer Extemporay* and in the year following, *A Discourse of the Liberty of Prophesying*. The former was later expanded into *An Apology for Authorized and Set Forms of Liturgie* which was published in 1649. Though it was said that *The Liberty of Prophesying* did not please the king, it is worth noting that Charles later included Taylor's name amongst those of his chaplains whom he desired to see while he was in prison, and Taylor was consulted with others as to whether a prince might tolerate religions other than the one established within his kingdom.

In 1649 Taylor seems to have tired of controversy. He admits that he is 'weary and toiled with rowing up and down in the seas of questions, which the interests of Christendom have commenced'.[1] He made his first attempt to produce a book of popular piety, *The Great Exemplar*. Interwoven with the story of the life of Christ are practical exhortations. The intellectual arguments of the day are replaced by suggestions for developing the life of individual piety. 'I have chosen', he says, 'to serve the purposes of religion by doing assistance to that part of theology which is wholly practical; that which makes us wiser therefore because it makes us better.'[2] The best known of his devotional works followed in 1650 and 1651: *The Rule and Exercises of Holy Living* and *The Rule and Exercises of Holy Dying*. The latter was written at the request of Lady Carbery before her untimely death in 1651. In passing we may note that Taylor's sermon (printed a year later) on the occasion of the funeral of this saintly woman is a model of this kind of oration. Further works appeared in the years following: *Clerus Domini* (1651), *A Discourse on Baptism* (1652), *A Short Catechism* (1652) which was later enlarged into *The Golden Grove* (1655). Two short works, one on Baptism and the other on Prayer appeared in 1653 and, more important perhaps, two volumes of sermons, later combined under the title *Eniautos, A Course of Sermons for All the Sundays of the Year*. Though not topical either from the viewpoint of current events or the Church calendar, they have a grace and beauty of their own. They were preached in the private chapel at Golden Grove, to those who had acquired a spiritual taste for all the counsel and instruction that Taylor could give them with such charm and eloquence.

Though he doubtless made journeys to London in connection with the publication of his books, from 1653 Taylor's visits were more frequent. In the year following he began a friendship with John Evelyn and became his spiritual counsellor. In 1654, *The Real Presence and Spiritual of Christ in the Blessed Sacrament* was published, to be followed a year later by *The Golden Grove* and *Unum Necessarium*. *The Golden Grove*

---

[1] *Works*, II, p. 3.   [2] *ibid.*, p. 2.

which was critical of the Independents brought about Taylor's imprisonment.

If this book aroused opposition from without Anglicanism, *Unum Necessarium* brought criticism from within. The chief cause of the trouble was a chapter on Original Sin in which Taylor expressed views that were considered to be strongly anti-Augustinian. Though the book contained a preface to Warner, Bishop of Rochester and Duppa, Bishop of Salisbury these prelates were not at all sensible of the honour that their old friend intended. They and others such as Sheldon and Sanderson were most disturbed. Samuel Rutherford, who had bitterly assailed *The Liberty of Prophesying* hastened to attack this new heresy. The book appeared while Taylor was undergoing a second imprisonment (this time at Chepstow Castle) and this increased the difficulty of the author in explaining his views. The publication of correspondence in which Taylor elaborated his beliefs and even the issue of *Deus Justificatus* (a lengthy letter to the Countess Dowager of Devonshire which his publisher obtained and printed without his permission) did not remove the suspicion of Pelagianism. It is highly probable that the book which Taylor wrote in the hope of urging people to repentance and holiness of life was the cause of his failure to obtain an English bishopric.

Taylor's wife had died in 1651 but after his release from Chepstow he married Joanna Bridges and lived at Mandinam. All Taylor's biographers have assumed that his second wife was a woman of property who owned Mandinam in the parish of Llangadog, Co. Carmarthen, but according to deeds in the Glensevin Collection at the National Library of Wales, this property at Mandinam was purchased in July 1660, by Jeremy, his wife Joane and his daughter Johanna from George Gwynne. Here he lost a boy of his second marriage and six months later two sons of his first marriage. It was while he was at Mandinam that he began to prepare his *magnum opus*, *Ductor Dubitantium*, to which in one sense *Unum Necessarium* had been a preface.

In 1657 Taylor returned to London where he not only ministered to private congregations of royalists but visited individuals and groups at some distance from the city. It has been suggested that he was in demand not only as a preacher but as a spiritual director to the many who appreciated his pastoral as well as his pulpit gifts. This must have been a time of particular peril for an Anglican clergyman. He suffered a third imprisonment but Evelyn used his influence to secure his release. Though Taylor would be busy, he was able to respond to the request of Mrs Katharine Phillips, a woman of high literary attainments, about the Christian attitude to friendship. He produced a small book entitled *A Discourse of the Nature and Offices of Friendship*. The year following Taylor published his *Collection of Offices*, which he believed might be an acceptable substitute for the *Book of Common Prayer* which was now forbidden. Taylor like other royalists hoped optimistically for toleration if the Prayer Book was not pressed too vigorously. In 1658 another son was born who did not survive.

After twelve years in universities and twenty fraught with uncertainty, Taylor came to the last stage of his life. During his time in London he had become friendly with the Conway family who had considerable estates in Northern Ireland. It was arranged that Taylor should go as chaplain to the Conway household at Portmore. About eight miles away at Lisburn (formerly Lisnagarvey) lived Major Rawdon, Conway's brother-in-law. The family in Ireland had endured for some time the ministrations of Andrew Wyke, an Anabaptist, who had been installed by the Government. Conway wrote to influential people in Ireland to prepare the way for Taylor for he was not *persona grata* with all in authority there. Taylor was given together with letters of recommendation to important persons, a pass for himself and his family under Cromwell's sign manual and privy signet.[1]

For some months Taylor lived alternately at Lisburn and Portmore but then settled at the latter place and sent for

---

[1] *Rawdon Papers*, Conway to Rawdon, June 15th, 1658.

his two daughters who had been left in England. Evelyn who had helped him before financially did not forget him now; he was one of the few of his old friends who continued to correspond. Taylor was making new friends in Ireland, of course, and he had his book on Conscience to complete which must have taken a good deal of his time. Even in the quiet of Portmore he was not safe from criticism; he was accused of using the sign of the cross in baptizing a child. Many Presbyterians from Scotland had settled in Ireland; the arrival of a man with Taylor's reputation was not likely to please.

Taylor finished writing *Ductor Dubitantium* in 1660 and took it to London to his publisher Royston. He arrived in time to join in the welcome to Charles II on May 29th. His book was dedicated to the king. It is possible that he hoped for an English bishopric. But the author of *The Liberty of Prophesying* and *Unum Necessarium* was suspect. He was nominated by the king on August 6th as bishop of the diocese of Down and Connor and shortly afterwards was made Vice-Chancellor of the University of Dublin. Before he left England Taylor completed *The Worthy Communicant*.

The state of the Anglican Church in Ireland was chaotic. Roman Catholicism had always had a strong hold on the people and the Reformation had made but little impression on the life of the country as a whole; two-thirds of the population still gave their primary allegiance to the Pope. The influx of Presbyterians during the persecution in Scotland had produced a forceful minority which was as antagonistic to Canterbury as to Rome. Rather naturally, these immigrants had settled in that part of Ireland which was nearest to Scotland, so that a number were to be found in Taylor's diocese. To them, in any event, episcopacy was distasteful; to make matters worse, they were already acquainted with the views of the new bishop. As if opposition within his diocese were not enough, Taylor had also to face problems confronting him in Dublin University. Its affairs were far from satisfactory. Taylor began by legalizing the

constitution, remodelling the statutes and by various un-
spectacular acts established the University in a proper
manner. The present high regard in which it is held is due
in part to the sound way in which Taylor relaid its foundations. Difficult as this task was, it was undoubtedly easier
than trying to create some sort of order in his diocese.

The remaining period of Taylor's life was not happy;
failing health and troubles with the Presbyterians left their
mark. Adair has said truly that had Taylor been removed
from this world before he reached the episcopal throne he
would have left a far more savoury reputation.[1] It was, of
course, hard for those who opposed him to regard Taylor as
other than a persecutor. Both Presbyterians and Anglicans
were men of strong convictions, and the economic as well as
the propaganda value of the holding of livings was inextricably bound up with the questions at issue.

The first shot in the battle was fired by the Presbyterians
who examined the writings of Taylor and declared them to
be heretical. Taylor appealed to Ormonde, Chancellor of
Dublin University, to be given aid or to be allowed to return
to England. He seems to have been given some promise of
help. He was consecrated as bishop in January 1661. When
he commanded the clergy to meet him at his Visitation, the
Presbyterians agreed to meet him privately but refused to
attend the Visitation. When they arrived the Presbyterians
stated they regarded their form of government as *jure divino*.
This made the bishop realize that there was really no hope
of compromise. Such an expert on cases of conscience was
bound to respect the convictions of his opponents, though he
could not tolerate them if they refused to obey the law.
Taylor declared their thirty-six livings vacant and sought to
fill them with men who were episcopally ordained. This was
a bitter blow to the Presbyterians but, in justice to Taylor,
it must be stated that he was not unreasonable in expecting
those who remained within Anglicanism to accept its order
and discipline. It is hard to see how he could have been

---

[1] P. Adair, *True Narrative*, p. 31.

faithful to his own conscience had he acted otherwise. To Taylor both Presbyterians and Jesuits were alike enemies of the king and the Church; as such he dealt with them according to his principles.

In February 1661, Taylor was made a member of the Irish Privy Council and in the June following was appointed administrator of the diocese of Dromore, though he was never to be its bishop. He contributed generously to the cost of rebuilding its ruined cathedral. The diocese of Down possessed no cathedral so the parish church at Lisburn was designated as such in 1662. Perhaps Dromore was added as a sop to Taylor for he had sought unsuccessfully to be translated to the diocese of Meath on the death of its bishop. On March 10th, 1661, his son Edward, probably born in 1659, was buried at Lisburn. In this year his *Rules and Advices to the Clergy of the Diocese of Down and Connor* was published.

Taylor's preaching was greatly admired and we still may read some of his sermons of this period, preached at Visitations, at the opening of the Irish Parliament, to the University of Dublin, at the consecration of Archbishops and Bishops in Dublin in 1660 as well as one on the duty of the clergy and one at the funeral of the Bishop of Armagh. In addition he published in 1664 his treatise on *Confirmation* and a *Dissuasive from Popery*, the second part of the latter appearing three years later.

An interesting story has survived about Taylor on the subject of the occult. This throws some light on his general attitude. A man named Taverner had been troubled by an apparition which said that he would have no rest until he promised to warn some people who were alleged to be defrauding the dead man's son. Taylor told Taverner to ask the apparition some practical questions: 'Whence are you? Are you a good or a bad spirit? Where is your abode? What station do you hold? How are you regimented in the other world? And what is the reason you appear for the relief of your son in so small a matter, when so many widows and orphans are oppressed in the world, being defrauded of greater matters, and none from thence of their relations appear, as you do, to right them?' Apparently this was too much for the spirit when it next appeared. 'It gave him no answer, but crawled on its hands and feet over the wall again, and so vanished in white with a most melodious harmony.'[1]

Taylor's last years, as has been indicated, were not happy. He wrote to Sheldon in 1664 pleading to be translated to an English diocese but this was denied him. His only surviving son Charles died in London at about the age of twenty-four early in August 1667. By the time this news reached Ireland Taylor was beyond further discouragement. He fell ill early in August and died in the afternoon of August 13th almost fifty-four years to the day from that on which he was baptized. His old friend George Rust preached the funeral sermon when Taylor was buried at Dromore on September 3rd, 1667.[2]

Though none of Taylor's sons survived him his three daughters lived on. There is no record of the marriage of his daughter Phoebe; Mary married Francis Marsh who afterwards became Archbishop of Dublin; Joanna married Edward Harrison who was later M.P. for Lisburn. Her daughter married Sir Cecil Wray and was the Lady Wray who it was alleged was responsible for writing in 1732 to Todd Jones, a distant relative of Taylor's, and suggesting that Joanna Bridges was the illegitimate child of Charles I. In spite of the acceptance of these stories by Heber and Mr Ross Williamson, the present writer feels that there is not sufficient evidence to include this and other stories connected with Lady Wray in a life of Taylor.

This brief biographical sketch may serve as a setting in which to study the piety of Jeremy Taylor. It shows both the breadth and the limitations of his experience. At first sight it might seem that so much of his life was spent in academic circles and with the aristocracy of his day that he was completely out of touch with those in less favourable circumstances.

[1] Glanvill, *Sadducimus Triumphatus*, Part 2, p. 234 ff.
[2] *Conway Letters*, p. 289.

While it is true that he was probably happiest with those in the former groups, we must not forget either his time at Uppingham or his chaplaincy in the Army. Comparatively short as these experiences were they brought him into touch with another side of life and, perhaps, recalled to him the days of his own childhood, for he was not born into an aristocratic family. He had his share of trouble in the loss of first wife and children and knew from experience the temptations that poverty brings. He suffered imprisonment, the misunderstanding of his friends and disappointment in his hopes. Like the distinguished prophet of the Old Testament whose name he bore, the circumstances of his life threw him back time and again upon God, and though like Jeremiah he was by nature timid, he learnt to become a strong pillar through recourse to Divine grace.

It has been suggested that Taylor had little knowledge of the strength of temptation to more passionate natures, that he addressed himself to Christians who like himself wished to grow in grace, rather than to those who were perplexed in mind or weak in will. It would be a mistake to read too much into such a judgement. His writings suggest that he had a real understanding of the ways of the human heart and a man of sympathetic insight may find himself at one with those whose temptations are not his own. Even if it be admitted that Taylor wrote mainly for the ordinary Christian who may know little of the depths of degradation or the heights of rapture, he would still have done a great service to the majority unacquainted with the extremes.

Taylor's skill as a writer of English prose, his erudition and wide knowledge of the classics and the Fathers, his theological learning and comprehension of ecclesiastical polity, even his churchmanship are not the primary preoccupation of this study. It is the piety of Taylor that is our chief concern; these other attributes only find a place as they contribute to this aspect of his life and thought. Taylor lived in an age of spiritual giants and he is not unworthy to be included amongst the greatest of them. Every school of thought at that time produced its saints; unfortunately, their divergencies were such that they failed to realize that in piety they were near to each other. Coleridge, in an extended comparison of Milton and Taylor, makes clear their differences but says that they agreed 'in genius, in learning, in unfeigned piety, in blameless purity of life, and in benevolent aspirations and purposes for moral and temporal improvement of their fellow-creatures'.[1]

Rust concludes his funeral sermon on Taylor with these words: 'This great prelate he had the good humour of a gentleman, the eloquence of an orator, the fancy of a poet, the acuteness of a school-man, the profoundness of a philosopher, the wisdom of a counsellor, the sagacity of a prophet, the reason of an angel and the piety of a saint. He had devotion enough for a cloister, learning enough for an university, and wit enough for a college of *virtuosi;* and had his parts and endowments been parcelled out among his poor clergy that he left behind him, it would perhaps have made one of the best dioceses in the world.'[2]

[1] Coleridge, *Miscellanies*, p. 210 ff.   [2] *Works*, I, p. cccxxvii.

Chapter Two

THEOLOGICAL POSITION

<>◇<>

In order to understand Taylor's piety it is necessary to give a brief account of his general theological outlook. While he had much in common with his Anglican contemporaries there were, as has been hinted, certain points on which he differed. There are some whose maturer thoughts are simply an expansion of earlier basic ideas; Taylor is not so consistent. He was by nature susceptible; maturity, in his case, was marked by modifications in outlook which arose as much from changing circumstances as from increase in years. We may assume that he was a loyal son of the Church of England who accepted the historic Creeds and the Thirty-Nine Articles, and draw attention to four aspects of the Faith where he has made an individual contribution.

I. THE MINISTRY

Taylor was reared in an Anglicanism which had had to find its own distinctive ethos since the Reformation. 'Reformation' suggests a reconstruction of constitutive elements rather than a revolutionary overthrowing of the old to make way for the new. In reply to accusations of innovations in theology and polity, Anglican reformers stressed that they were retaining the teachings of the Bible, as well as the faith and practice of the primitive Church, purged of Roman accretions.

The Elizabethan Settlement ensured national unity at the expense of diminishing the authority of the clergy. They, with the sovereign and laity, were to combine in working out the practical system of the English Church. The attempt made by Elizabeth to base the Prayer Book and Articles upon the authority of the Crown (acting on the advice of Convocation) was successfully resisted by the Houses of Parliament. This did nothing to remove ambiguity from the sovereign's title of Supreme Governor. The Calvinists could and did appeal to the authority of their *Institutes*, the Romanists to the Pope and the Council of Trent; Anglicans had to discover their own authority and evolve their theological and ecclesiastical position by what must have seemed to others hasty improvisation. Our native genius for compromise and the *via media* is exemplified nowhere more clearly than in the development of Anglicanism in the years following its severance from Rome.

James in his familiar dictum 'No bishop, no king' linked the monarchy and episcopacy inextricably together. That it had certain advantages needs no elaboration. If Father Pope was no longer to be the guardian of the national Church, there was precedent enough in Isaiah's prophecy that kings should be nursing-fathers and queens nursing-mothers. The idea of the 'godly prince' was developed and expanded from this and other Old Testament passages. If the idea gave not unwelcome support to the authority of the king, what of the bishop? In Europe as a whole episcopacy had fallen into disrepute because of bad examples furnished by the Roman Church; some countries abandoned it either deliberately or through force of circumstances, though Luther and Calvin were not completely opposed to the theory. Criticism at home and abroad led Anglicans to a careful examination of the place of episcopal succession, not only in respect of doctrine but of office. Early claims based the episcopacy on apostolical rather than dominical institution. Professor Sykes has said: 'Under the pressure of a century of acute controversy the Anglican divines had developed a positive constructive and consistent apologetic for episcopacy as retained in the Church of England. It was held to be not of dominical but apostolic appointment, and *divino jure* only in that sense.'[1]

During the reign of Charles I, the growing strength of the Puritan element and increasing opposition to Laud's policy of Thorough, culminating in the Root and Branch petition, threatened the bastion of episcopacy until it seemed to men like Taylor to be in danger of complete collapse. There were even waverers amongst the faithful. The impeachment of Laud and growing hostility to the throne must have made James's 'no bishop, no king' seem unpleasantly prophetic. *Episcopacy Asserted* is not therefore to be regarded so much as a thesis for the Doctorate that Taylor was awarded as a result of it but rather as a Tract for the Times.

If this was the book's purpose we should not assume that it was over hastily put together; it deals with the subject at length and in great detail. Taylor bases his claim for the foundation of episcopacy on divine institution, apostolic tradition and catholic practice. In dealing with the first he asserts that it cannot have arisen from human prudence, convenience or new circumstances: 'To trust such a rich commodity in a cock-boat that no wise pilot will be supposed to do.'[2] Divine institution is supported, he claims, by the authority given to the apostles to bind and to loose, and the 'faithful and wise steward' in St. Luke's gospel is additional evidence since steward is synonymous with pastor and pastor means ruler.

Canon Stranks, after summarizing Taylor's argument, says: 'Having proved the divine origin of bishops Taylor goes on to seek the origin of the presbyterate.'[3] But though Taylor has certainly gone further than most of his contemporaries in claiming episcopacy to be of dominical institution, we may question whether he has in fact proved it. He shifts his ground fifteen years later when he writes a second dedicatory preface to try to reconcile the different views expressed in *Episcopacy Asserted* and *The Liberty of Prophesying*.

[1] N. Sykes, *Old Priest and New Presbyter*, p. 81.   [2] *Works*, V, p. 16.
[3] C. J. Stranks, *The Life and Writings of Jeremy Taylor*, p. 57.

Here he makes episcopacy rely 'not upon the authority of fathers and councils, but upon scripture, upon the institution of Christ, *or the institution of the apostles*, upon an universal tradition and on universal practice, not upon the words and opinions of the doctors'.[1] Canon Stranks quotes this passage but rather curiously omits the words I have italicized and gives no reason for doing so. In this same preface Taylor says that his emphasis on Fathers and Councils in *Episcopacy Asserted* was to help those who found them valuable. It would appear that in *Episcopacy Asserted* Taylor went further than most in the matter of dominical institution but became more cautious in later years.

Taylor is in line with other Anglicans in placing the bishop above the presbyter when he states: 'Although we had not proved the immediate divine institution of episcopal power over presbyters and the whole flock, yet episcopacy is not less than an apostolical ordinance, and delivered us by the same authority that the observation of the Lord's day is.' He thinks that it should therefore be included in the *credenda* of Christianity.[2] He does not hesitate to find the origin of the presbyterate in the commission given to the seventy, nor to include in their ranks Ananias (who baptized St. Paul), Philip the Evangelist, Judas (Justus) Silas, Mark, John the Presbyter and the seven deacons. In order to circumvent criticisms that they too were ordained by Christ, and could therefore claim equality with the apostles, Taylor suggests that though they received the rest of the power through the apostles the commission to preach only was given by Christ.[3] There are of course obvious difficulties in these claims. We have no proof that any of those named were in fact amongst the seventy, neither is Taylor convincing in making such sharp distinctions between bishops and presbyters in New Testament times. He explains the reference to bishops in St. Paul's speech to the elders of Ephesus by suggesting that either other bishops came from the province, or that there may have been more than one bishop at Ephesus or, most

[1] *Works*, V, p. 4.   [2] *ibid.*, p. 68 f.   [3] *ibid.*, p. 38.

probably he thinks, those who came from Ephesus were consecrated bishops at Miletus.[1] This is a good example of the kind of reasoning of which Taylor at times was capable.

The argument from apostolic tradition for the superiority of bishops Taylor illustrates fully by quotations from the Fathers. The Presbyterians may claim the support of Jerome, but he counters this by saying that Jerome states that presbyters may not ordain. When Taylor comes to catholic practice he tells us that at first special offices had particular names; bishop was the exclusive name for the ruler of the Church. The bishop is the guarantee of unity and to him is given authority over clergy and laity. He expresses similar views to the above in the Consecration Sermon preached at Dublin in 1660.[2]

Writing in 1661 on the ministry in general, Taylor asserts that there have always been some set apart to minister in holy things. To have experts in other spheres of life and to be without them in the spiritual is to offer a dishonourable religion to God.[3] Christians must not do less than Jews and Gentiles who set apart the noblest to be priests. He stresses both the duty and the office when he says: 'When Christ had chosen to Himself twelve apostles, and was drawing now to the last scene of His life, He furnished them with commissions and abilities to constitute and erect a church, and to transmit such powers as were apt for its continuation and perpetuity.'[4]

This ministry has power to bind and to loose, to preach the gospel and administer the sacraments. Though Taylor recognized that Priscilla and the daughters of Philip were women who were allowed to prophesy and that Aquila and Agabus were laymen, he says: 'These will be but too strait an argument to blend a whole order of men in a popular and vulgar indiscrimination.'[5] So strongly does he feel the need for ordination that he is not prepared for laymen to baptize; to do so might open the door to their doing other work which

[1] *ibid.*, V, p. 77.   [2] *ibid.*, VIII, p. 305 ff.   [3] *ibid.*, I, p. 6 f.
[4] *ibid.*, I, p. 11.   [5] *ibid.*, I, p. 17.

c

belongs to the ministry.[1] We can assume from *Clerus Domini*
that there was little change in his views over twenty years.

Taylor of course was not unaware of the discussions taking
place both at home and abroad on the subject of the rival
merits of different ecclesiastical systems. In *Episcopacy Asserted*
he asks the question: 'What think we of the reformed
churches? For my part I know not what to think; the question
hath been so often asked, with so much violence and prejudice, and we are so bound by public interest to approve all
that they do, that we disabled ourselves to justify our own.
For we were glad at first of these abettors against the Roman
church; we found these men zealous in it; we thanked God
for it, as we had cause; and we were willing to make them
recompense by endeavouring to justify their own ordinations,
not thinking what would follow upon ourselves; but now it
is come to that issue that our own episcopacy is thought not
necessary because we did not condemn the ordinations of
their presbytery. Why is not the question rather what we
think of the primitive church than what we think of the
reformed churches?'[2]

Taylor becomes more aggressive as he states that the
presbyterian model of ordination has no support from
Scripture or antiquity which, he says, come down on the
side of episcopal ordination. While others had excused
differences in order and lack of episcopal ordination in view
of the necessity of the times, Taylor asks whether it was really
necessary for some countries to abolish it. He mentions
critically the practice current in France of reordaining those
who had returned to their native country, even though they
had received episcopal ordination. 'The want of a bishop
will not excuse us from our endeavours of acquiring one.'[3]
Though he will not utterly condemn those churches which
have no bishops, he feels that they are like the church of
Pergamus — there are 'some few things' which Christ has

---

[1] *Works*, I, p. 29 f. Taylor says in *Episcopacy Asserted* that baptism by laymen
is valid, 'but yet they ought not to administer it.' (V, p. 153 f.)
[2] *ibid.*, V, p. 118.   [3] *ibid.*, p. 120.

against them. All this suggests that Taylor was more rigid than some of his contemporaries and predecessors in his attitude to episcopacy. Nevertheless, we must bear in mind the circumstances that produced *Episcopacy Asserted* and the aggressive opposition he encountered in Ireland to episcopal authority.

2. TOLERATION

'The Anglican ideal as expressed by Chillingworth and Hales and attempted by Laud was the truly Catholic ideal not of the toleration of churches, but of a tolerant church . . . The one thing which could not be tolerated was active intolerance in any form, a limitation not peculiar to Anglicanism.'[1] This judgement of Haller's may be set alongside another which illustrates the unyielding temper of the Puritans: 'The church according to them was absolutely authoritative over religious opinion no less than religious practice. It could tolerate no difference of creed. The distinction between fundamental and non-fundamental articles of belief, elaborately maintained by Chillingworth and Taylor, was held to be dangerous heresy; and the principle of latitude, with all the essential idea of free thought which has sprung out of it, was esteemed unchristian.'[2] From what we have seen of his views in *Episcopacy Asserted*, it may seem strange to find Taylor's name included in the second quotation. Yet in 1647 he produced a work entitled *The Liberty of Prophesying* on the subject of toleration which was far ahead of the general thought of his own day. This claim is supported by a letter from an Independent of that century, Roger Williams, in a letter to Mrs Sadleir, daughter of Sir Edward Coke. Taylor, he asserted, 'excellently asserted the toleration of different religions, yea, in a respect, that of the papists themselves, which is a new way of soul freedom, and yet is the old way

---

[1] W. Haller, *The Rise of Puritanism*, p. 247.
[2] J. Tulloch, *Rational Theology and Christian Philosophy in England in the 17th Century*, II, p. 4.

of Christ Jesus.' Mrs Sadlier was not impressed; *The Liberty of Prophesying* was not to her stomach. 'I say,' she replied, 'it and you would make a good fire.'[1]

The general spirit of this lengthy work may be summed up in one extract: 'If the persons be Christians in their lives and Christians in their profession, if they acknowledge the eternal Son of God for their Master and their Lord, and live in all relations as becomes persons making such professions, why then should I hate such persons whom God loves and who love God, who are partakers of Christ and Christ hath a title to them, who dwell in Christ and Christ in them, because their understandings have not been brought up like mine, have not had the same masters, they have not met with the same books nor the same company, or have not the same interest, or are not so wise, or else are wiser . . . have not the same opinions that I have, and do not determine their school-questions to the sense of my sect or interest?'[2]

Taylor naturally will not give encouragement to the kind of religion that is contrary to a good life or the Christian faith, or is anarchical, but in doubtful things he counsels liberty. For four hundred years after Christ, he tells us, very few Christians ever sought secular power to help them against heretics. It did occur in the case of Arius for a time, 'but', he adds grimly, 'it was soon taken off, and God left to be his judge; who indeed did it to some purpose, when He was trusted with it.'[3] Each Church has its differences — Roman, Greek, Lutheran, Zwinglian, Calvinist, Anabaptist or Nestorian: 'To pitch upon any one of these is to throw the dice, if salvation be to be had only in one of them, and that every error that by chance hath made a sect, and is distinguished by a name, be damnable.'[4] Questions like predestination and the efficacy of death-bed repentances are more important than the existence of purgatory or the validity of masses, yet they have not produced sects.

[1] Cited by W. K. Jordan: *The Development of Religious Toleration in England*, III, p. 505.
[2] *Works*, V, p. 346.   [3] *ibid.*, p. 350.   [4] *ibid.*, p. 355 ff.

The Apostles' Creed is a summary, Taylor says, of all that is necessary for belief. He regrets the extensions of creeds that took place from Nicea onwards, underestimating perhaps the reasons that led to their promulgation: 'If the apostles admitted all to their communion that believed this creed, why should we exclude any that preserve the same entire?'[1] Taylor seeks to show at some length the insufficiency of Councils, Popes and Fathers in solving knotty points and stresses the necessity for liberty in interpretation of the disputable passages of Scripture. This brings him to the point where he is bound to stress the importance of reason in showing us how to express our piety and love to God and truth.[2] Reason Taylor would not define as the mind of man alone: '(It is) not guided only by natural arguments but by divine revelation and all other good means.'[3]

In dealing with those who are in honest disagreement Taylor urges that 'no Christian is to be put to death, dismembered or otherwise directly persecuted for his opinion, which does not teach impiety or blasphemy.'[4] Though treason and sedition must be punished there is always a danger that compulsion will breed hypocrisy or lead the persecuted to charge their opponents with bolstering up weak arguments with force of arms. Two particular parties are selected as examples of those to whom toleration could be extended. He deals with the view of the Anabaptists at some length and, though he is critical of their dogmas, he is prepared to grant them toleration. What is even more surprising, in view of the prevailing attitude, is that he is also willing, with proper safeguards, to include the Romans.

Taylor's impassioned plea for tolerance arose from his concern for holiness which he realized was wider than any particular Church. It is reinforced on this basis in *Holy Living* where he suggests that the spiritual quality of the Church is more important than 'uninterrupted succession of bishops'. It is referred to again in the sermon *Via Intelligentiae*

---

[1] *ibid.*, p. 373. [2] *ibid.*, p. 409-99. [3] *ibid.*, p. 495.
[4] *ibid.*, p. 514.

preached in 1662, fifteen years after the writing of *The Liberty of Prophesying* when he was himself a bishop. Yet his great attempt to explore the meaning of catholicity has been dismissed on the one hand as too accommodating and on the other as motivated by self-interest.

One of the severest of Taylor's critics is Mr Ross Williamson who regards *The Liberty of Prophesying* as a piece of special pleading, adapted to the particular situation during the struggle between the King, Parliament and the Army. Taylor, he tells us, wrote in the spirit of a casuistical Erastian rather than as a prophet of liberty.[1] If this is a valid point we ought to know why it was that Taylor (who was quite unsympathetic to the Roman viewpoint) included a plea for the toleration of Roman Catholics as well as Anabaptists; while the latter might be classed with Independents the former were not a party to the triangular struggle. Again, if this is special pleading suited to a particular situation, why when circumstances altered in favour of the Church of England does he (with but slight modifications) reiterate the same principles in *Via Intelligentiae* and why does he accuse the Roman Catholics and Calvinists of using the very methods with which Mr Williamson charges him? Why does the Apostles' Creed as being the only necessary rule of faith appear again twenty years after *The Liberty of Prophesying* in the second half of the *Dissuasive from Popery* which was published in the year of Taylor's death? In that work he states: 'English Protestants deny not their communion to any who desires it, and believes the apostles' creed, and is of the religion of the four first general councils; they hope well of all that live well; they receive into their bosom all true believers of what church soever, and for them that err, they instruct them, and then leave them to their liberty, to stand or fall before their own Master.'[2]

In attacking the substance of the book Mr Williamson alleges that Taylor included safeguards which allowed 'the Catholics and the Dissenters to be denied on political

[1] H. Ross Williamson, *Jeremy Taylor*, p. 45 ff.   [2] *Works*, VI, p. 478 f.

grounds the liberty conceded to them on religious should the Church of England ever be re-established'. This is, of course, a possible interpretation; it is equally possible that Taylor was expressing his views in the context of his belief in law and order and distinguishing between liberty and licence. Even to-day tolerance has its limitations; expressions of opinion that lead to a breach of the peace are not permitted. It would be even more necessary in the seventeenth century to make the position clear.

Mr Ross Williamson is most critical of Taylor's theological argument. He thinks that the Apostles' Creed is meaningless apart from the interpretations which were later attached to its clauses: 'Interpretation, if it is to be anything but individualism, presupposes an authoritative interpreter and at that point the stubborn dividing question appears once more. What in fact is the Church?' To answer the question we must look at it in the light of Taylor's Arminianism. The Puritans and Arminians both believed the Scriptures to be supremely authoritative; the former regarded the Bible as having a constraining power *over* the reason and conscience. The Arminians felt the authority of Scripture to be 'directive'. It is the witness of the Holy Spirit in the Divine word; but it can only be brought near to the individual and become operative by his own free enquiry and assent.[1] Because Taylor took this attitude he was bound to incur the wrath of Puritans and the disagreement of some members of his own party.

Yet it would be unfair to Taylor to assume that in *The Liberty of Prophesying* he disparages the authority of Scripture. He may limit it in matters of disputation and show that where men differ it cannot be quoted to settle the argument finally, but that it is the supreme authority in things essential, and that its teaching (summarized in the Apostles' Creed) is the irreducible minimum are stressed in the *Dissuasive from Popery* as well as the *Liberty of Prophesying*. Other authorities

[1] J. Tulloch, *Rational Theology and Christian Philosophy in England in the Seventeenth Century*, Vol. I, p. 28.

occupy a secondary place and are only to be followed in so far as they conform to the Bible. To those who glorify tradition, Taylor brings the testimony of tradition to the Bible as a full and sufficient rule for the Christian in faith and manners, a full and perfect declaration of the will of God. If he is criticized because he seems to make the ultimate authority private judgement, we must remind ourselves that he does not think of reason apart from revelation. Those who are suspicious of private judgement and raise the bogey of individualism sometimes forget that it is by private judgement, in the final analysis, that man chooses his ultimate authority.

In concluding this estimate of Taylor's contribution, we ought to look briefly at his attitude to communion with other churches. It has been suggested, particularly by Canon Brown, that in what Taylor wrote on this subject he meant nothing more than fellowship and goodwill, certainly not 'inter-communion', in the sense that the Eucharist should be offered to those who have not conformed to the discipline of the Church of England. He thinks that Taylor believes this to be so because of the laws obtaining in different churches.[1] But is the matter as simple as Canon Brown would have us believe? Taylor uses the words 'communion' and 'communicate' ambiguously; at different times they may mean either Holy Communion or fellowship. Taylor's statement that it is wrong 'to deny to communicate with those whom God has vouchsafed to be united, and refuse our charity to those who have the same faith', Canon Brown interprets as meaning mutual toleration. But Taylor, in the section referred to, speaks of Anicetus and Polycarp being charitable to each other; this certainly involved Polycarp not only being present at the Communion, but celebrating.

Taylor's later views do not contradict this interpretation of 'communion' in *The Liberty of Prophesying*. Anglicans may not communicate in Huguenot churches with them that

[1] W. J. Brown, *Jeremy Taylor* (English Theologians), p. 63 ff. and 83.

believe episcopacy to be antichristian or unlawful because in effect it breaks English national law. Yet a subject of the Church of England may stand at Holy Communion or eat it in leavened bread, if he is attending the celebration in a country which has that custom.[1] This surely presupposes more than passive attendance.

That Communion could be given to those outside the discipline of the Church of England, Taylor states quite definitely in *Ductor Dubitantium*, as well as in the passage from the *Dissuasive from Popery* cited above.[2] In the former work, alongside his statement that he will not himself receive the elements from a man ordained by a presbyter, he says: 'I will not refuse to give him the communion if he will require it at my hand.'[3] It is sometimes forgotten that the Church of England then took a rather wider view than she does now towards receiving as communicants those who had not been episcopally confirmed. Casaubon was of the French congregation but he was even promised a prebend stall at Canterbury and Bishop Andrewes gave him the Sacrament when he was dying. As Bishop Henson says: 'He (Casaubon) certainly never received the rite of episcopal confirmation nor episcopal ordination, nor had he submitted to Anglican formularies. There was nothing extraordinary in all this, and it did not attract any special notice.'[4] The law that made occasional conformity a necessary qualification for a place in the magistracy shows that objection on the ground that the individual had not been confirmed was not considered to be a bar by the Church authorities. Even a century later there were Methodists (many of whom had not been confirmed since until their conversion they were outside organized religion) who were attending Holy Communion in their parish churches without exception being taken to their presence, nor was enquiry made about their attitude to Anglican formularies. If Taylor cannot be cited as an

---

[1] *Works*, X, p. 60 f.   [2] *ibid.*, VI, p. 478 f.   [3] *ibid.*, X, p. 310 f.
[4] H. Henson, *English Religion in the Seventeenth Century*, p. 25 f. See also the same author's *The Church of England*, p. 114 ff.

apostle of 'inter-communion', his attitude is broader than that of some Anglicans to-day.

In spite of the militancy of his opponents in Ireland and the difficulties that beset Taylor in governing his diocese, it is greatly to his credit that in that period we should find echoes of *The Liberty of Prophesying* in his writings. Even if Taylor can be charged with modifying his opinions, his great work on toleration was far ahead of its time. No doubt it owed something to Chillingworth, Hales and Daille, but the spirit of the book is Taylor's own. It may be that he lacked the necessary systematic thought to follow up all its implications, yet what began as a suggested way of toleration possibly opened up such vistas to Taylor that he was carried beyond the horizons of his own age to a vision of something greater. He caught a glimpse of the Church that was greater than the barriers which divided the Christian from his brother. Because of his own love of holiness he saw the Church not so much as an organization but as a brotherhood, in which each was united to the other through his love of Christ. For Taylor, the Holy, Catholic Church is the communion of saints; the second term describes the first. In the second part of his *Dissuasive from Popery* he says: 'The apostles have in the creed comprehended all the christian world, all the congregation of Christ's servants in the world "catholic".' And a little later he reminds us that God has by His wise providence 'preserved the plain places of scripture, and the apostles' creed in all churches to be the rule and measure of that faith by which the churches are saved, and which is the only means of the unity of Spirit, which is the band of peace in matters of belief.'[1] If Taylor has done nothing else, in *The Liberty of Prophesying* he has reminded us that Christ is more important than Christianity, the truth of the gospel of more significance than the disputations of ecclesiastics, and the Catholic Church wider than denominational differences.

[1] *Works*, VI, p. 349 ff.

3. ORIGINAL SIN

Ironically, Taylor's passion for piety and his desire to perfect men in holiness led to misunderstandings which were to discredit him in the eyes of friend and foe. The man who drew the line more rigidly than many between mortal and venial sin, and practically denied the value of a death-bed repentance (in that it gave too little time for that repentance to become effective) was accused of dangerous leanings to Pelagianism. Yet it was in protest against an attitude which lessened man's moral responsibility that Taylor wrote *Unum Necessarium*.

Taylor's controversial view on the subject of Original Sin appeared first in the sixth chapter of *Unum Necessarium*. The misunderstandings that arose compelled him to publish *A Further Explication of the Doctrine of Original Sin* which was included as the seventh chapter in subsequent editions of *Unum Necessarium*. In addition we have his correspondence with Warner, Bishop of Rochester, and Henry Jeanes of Chedzoy and the less technical *Deus Justificatus* which repeats earlier arguments in simpler terms.

The doctrine of Original Sin is a subject on which there has been much speculation. To put it very briefly: Augustinian teaching left man as a result of the Fall stripped not only of his supernatural power but with a greatly enfeebled will; it also emphasized the solidarity of fallen mankind. Those who followed the relentless logic of Calvin's interpretation of Augustine regarded man with the utmost pessimism. He was totally depraved, and only the elect (or select) few would be saved by the grace of God which was sometimes depicted as being irresistible. Taylor saw the dangers implicit in such a view. His own definition of Original Sin is that it is 'the sin of Adam which was committed in the original of mankind by our first parents, and which had influence upon all his posterity'. Death was the result, and Adam begat sons and daughters 'in the proper temper and constitution of mortal men'. He agrees that Adam lost certain graces and

was left in a natural state in which it was not possible for him
to attain a supernatural by his own efforts; he denies that
Adam's sin made it necessary for his descendants to sin,
'making it as natural to us to sin as to be hungry, or to be
sick and die.'[1]

One obvious criticism of Taylor's view was the apparently
opposite position taken by St Paul in Romans 5. There was
no thought in the seventeenth century of interpreting the
Apostle in the light of his Jewish background and any weakness in his argument was either unnoticed or disregarded.
Everything hinged on interpretation. Taylor explains the
passage as meaning that through Adam's disobedience we
were put into the order of sinners, and, because all have
sinned, we suffer death. Death, he says, becomes natural to
all but personal to all who sin. Man by his own choice turns
the imperfections of his nature into corruption. From Adam,
too, comes concupiscence which has been aggravated and
made worse by man's own acts. In general it would be fair
to say that Taylor stresses the negative aspect of the Fall —
man has lost something, but he is not endowed with guilt
and corruption until he chooses evil for himself. Adam lost
original righteousness but original guilt did not descend upon
his posterity: '(We) are left in our mere nature such as it
was, and such as it is.'[2]

How is it then that men are attracted to sin? Taylor points
out that in many instances men can and do by nature choose
and love the good, though this is not to imply that by nature
they know and love the supernatural excellencies which God
has appointed to bring them to a supernatural condition.
Apart from the grace of God men cannot be saved. There
are in addition certain contributory causes to the sinfulness
of men. Until the time of Christ the promises of God to mankind were restricted; if they had been given to Adam he
would not have fallen so easily. Secondly, God's laws
restrain the otherwise lawful and natural appetites. Rules of
temperance, abstinence, patience, humility, self-denial and

---

[1] *Works*, VII, p. 243 f.   [2] *ibid.*, p. 262.

mortification hedge us about. But our unwillingness to obey
cannot be attributed to Original Sin.[1]

Here Taylor has removed the blame from man only to
make God responsible. This was far from his intention, for
he goes on to show how man's freedom of will is demonstrated in that some choose sins which are abhorrent to
others. To say that a man has freedom only to sin, he asserts,
means that the precepts of holiness might as well be preached
to a wolf as a man. Freedom to choose can be limited through
consistent yielding to evil habits, but this is scarcely true of
any on all occasions. Man could certainly not be expected
to live a holy life if he were capable only of evil. He adds
that we accept this error to excuse ourselves.[2]

The further explanations that Taylor gives add little to
his general thesis. He regards Original Sin as a stain in its
effect. It does not destroy our natural liberty, nor introduce
a necessity of sinning, neither does it damn infants to the
pains of hell.[3] 'Every one talks of original sin, and agree that
there is such a thing, but what it is they agree not.'[4] This is
an interesting comment when we consider the history of this
doctrine. Taylor is quite sure that his teaching is not against
the Ninth Article of the Church of England (which in any
case is a general statement) and he quotes, as representing
his own position, the *Harmony of Confessions* printed at Cambridge in 1586 which, he says, was taken from the English
Confession inserted in the General Apology in 1562, the year
in which the Thirty-nine Articles were framed. If this
represents Taylor's position it will be useful to see what it
says: 'Every person is born in sin, and leadeth his life in sin,
and that nobody is able truly to say his heart is clean; and
that the most righteous person is but an unprofitable servant;
that the law of God is perfect, and requireth of us perfect
and full obedience; that we are able by no means to fulfil
that law in this worldly life; that there is no mortal creature
which can be justified by his own deserts in God's sight.'[5]

---

[1] *ibid.*, p. 276 f.   [2] *ibid.*, p. 281 ff.   [3] *ibid.*, p. 319 ff.
[4]*ibid.*, p. 330.   [5] *ibid.*, p. 331.

In some ways Taylor's views are more in accordance with modern teaching on the subject of Original Sin, in spite of some weaknesses in his arguments. In this connection a part of a modern statement is worth quoting: 'But we are committed to the view that humanity is now a *fallen humanity*, even though we no longer regard Genesis iii as giving us the actual account of the first "Fall". We may indeed regret that Augustine invented the misleading and inexact term "*original sin*." But we must certainly affirm the truth of experience to which Augustine applied the term — moral and spiritual weakness or handicap, the tendency towards evil rather than good, inherited by us all. . . . This weakness is a consequence of all the "actual" sins of mankind, just as in our own lives every lapse into sin reduces our powers of resistance against the next temptation.'[1]

Unum Necessarium, we must remind ourselves, was not intended as a controversial book but rather to call sinners to repentance. Nevertheless, once Taylor had stated his views he was prepared to defend them. If he could not find support for his ideas in Augustine, Aquinas or the Continental Reformers, he could appeal to some Eastern patristic writers, the Scotists and the Arminians who held a less gloomy view of humanity, and believed that man should rise to his responsibilities. Taylor's point that the Thirty-nine Articles gave a general statement of the faith within which there was liberty of interpretation is a good one. He is also on sure ground, from the point of view of urging men to repent, in laying stress on man's practical experience of sin rather than in theorizing about its origin, even though this may seem to involve a neglect of the powerful forces of heredity and racial solidarity of which more notice is taken to-day. We may be glad to note too in Taylor a revolt from that view of God which makes His character less worthy than that of good men. There are actions, as we know, attributed to God in the Old Testament for which modern Christians would not dream of holding Him responsible. Taylor was a child

[1] *Baptism Today*, p. 38 ff.

of his age; in this respect there was no attempt to give any but the usual interpretation. Where there was liberty he chose the larger view. One other point must be mentioned. It may be that the high rate of infant mortality, of which Taylor had experience in his home and outside, helped in contributing over the years to a wider view. His own kindly nature would make it difficult for him to contemplate infants being outside the mercy and care of their Heavenly Father.

4. THE SACRAMENTS

A. *Baptism*

The main sources for our knowledge of Taylor's views on Baptism are the sermon on this subject in *The Great Exemplar* and *The Liberty of Prophesying*. In the latter work in dealing with the toleration of the Anabaptists he devotes much space to answering their views. In his general attitude there is little to distinguish him from his Anglican contemporaries. One or two features are mentioned here to which reference will be made later. In *The Great Exemplar* Taylor speaks of a guardian angel being assigned to the child in Baptism and of the Holy Spirit coming to the infant as the principle of a new life. He stresses the need to bring the children to Christ and that the way is through the door of Baptism.

Through this sacrament we are born again, the effect of original sin is removed and we come within the covenant of grace: 'And therefore infants have a most certain capacity and proper disposition to baptism: for sin creeps before it can go; and little undecencies are soon learned, and malice is before their years, and they can do mischief and irregularities betimes; and though we know not when, nor how far, they are imputed in every month of their lives, yet it is an admirable art of the Spirit of grace, to put them into a state of pardon, that their remedy may at least be as soon as their necessity.'[1] Taylor feels that if parents neglect this sacrament, they must not be surprised if their offspring are not in heaven

[1] *Works*, II, p. 263.

to meet them. We need not follow the lengthy arguments
that he produced to confute the Anabaptists. Coleridge
summed the matter up when he said that the general effect
was to prove, if they proved anything, that both Taylor and
the Anabaptists were wrong and the Quakers only in the
right.[1] As we have seen in *Unum Necessarium* written six years
later than *The Great Exemplar*, Taylor is not happy about
infants being consigned to hell, and in *Clerus Domini* written
still later he is even firmer.[2]

Taylor's *Collection of Offices*, produced when the Prayer
Book was proscribed, contains a form of administration of
Baptism which differs somewhat from the 1662 *Book of
Common Prayer*. While the latter suggests that all men are
conceived and born in sin, Taylor omits this and says that
we derive nothing from our first parents but corruption. The
1662 Order speaks of the child receiving remission of sins
as though he had actually committed them; Taylor puts it
differently: 'We may therefore easily perceive that the
innocence of infants, and their freedom from actual sin,
cannot excuse them from baptism.'[3] This follows a statement
about our Lord being baptized, though He was innocent of
sin. Another interesting point about Taylor's Order is that
to the words 'I forsake them all', he adds 'and will be a
servant of Jesus Christ'. There is a prayer for God to send
His holy angel to be the guardian of the child against all
sorts of evils, including convulsions and rickets, mutilation
of a member and loss of sense.

The whole tone of Taylor's Order seems more in keeping
with modern ideas than that of 1662. It is less pessimistic in
tone and lays more stress on the part that the child will have
to play later. The assigning of the guardian angel at Baptism
is given prominence, and if we feel that it has some quaint
results (such as protecting the child from rickets) we have
perhaps in this age neglected an idea that has value in it.
Some of the things which he associates with Baptism, modern

---

[1] S. T. Coleridge, *Aids to Reflection*, p. 245.
[2] *Works*, I, p. 27.   [3] *ibid.*, VIII, p. 633.

Anglicans would be more inclined to link with the rite of Confirmation. His teaching that a child is capable of obtaining all the blessings of Baptism since there is nothing in him to hinder the grace of God, as there might be reservations in older people, fails to distinguish between the innocence of childhood and the mature sanctity of the experienced Christian. His difficulty, which is not his alone, is that he tends to apply passages in the Bible referring to adult Baptism to infants.

Taylor is optimistic in his claims for the efficacy of Baptism in infancy, and as the majority of those in that age were in closer touch with the Church than is now the case, perhaps he had some reason to be so. To-day when the situation has changed, we have realized the importance of the influence of the home and school in the religious development of the child. If the grace of God is to be limited to the channel of Baptism only it is hard to see why so few of those who are baptized come for Confirmation and why those who have never been baptized in infancy grow up to be loyal members of the Society of Friends, the Salvation Army or the Baptist Church. The more moderate words of the Lambeth Report give a fairer picture: 'We particularly value the practice of Infant Baptism for the emphasis which it lays upon the initiation of God in man's redemption, and in his translation from the kingdom of darkness into the kingdom of light, and also for the welcome which it gives to little children on their incorporation into the family of the Christian Church; but we do not claim for it the full meaning which the New Testament ascribes to adult initiation which includes Confirmation and First Communion.'[1]

B. *Confirmation*

As we have seen, there is a tendency in the Church of England to-day to link under one heading Baptism, Confirmation and First Communion. It is not therefore inappropriate at this point to give some account of

[1] *Baptism Today*, p. 19 and 37 f.

D

Taylor's teaching about the rite of Confirmation. His treatise on this subject was published in 1664 and compared with his other writings is remarkably succinct. It has been described as 'the greatest of all English books' on this subject. [1]

It has been pointed out by Dom Gregory Dix that in the primitive Church Confirmation was part of the sacrament of Initiation, being closely linked with Baptism. With the separation of the two in later times there was a tendency to regard Confirmation merely as strengthening the grace received in Baptism. Canon Quick provides a different approach when he states that Baptism confers the gift of the indwelling Spirit, and feels that Confirmation cannot be called a prime necessity of the Christian life. Where does Taylor stand? In his introduction to the treatise he speaks of the Spirit being at work in Baptism and repentance and many other facets of the spiritual life, but the general impression left is that it is at Confirmation that we receive the gift of the Holy Spirit 'as the earnest of our inheritance, as the seal of our salvation'. [2]

Taylor would not have the support of most scholars in finding the origin of Confirmation (which he does not call a sacrament) in the anointing of Christ by the Holy Spirit at His Baptism and in the words of our Lord to Nicodemus about being born of water and the Spirit. To separate 'water' and 'spirit' would not command general assent to-day. He finds further support for his views in the confirmation of Philip's work at Samaria by Peter and John, Paul laying his hands on the men at Ephesus that they might receive the Holy Spirit and the reference to laying on of hands in Hebrews 6. We may notice in passing, as Taylor did not, that the men at Ephesus had received only the baptism of John. He claims support for his views from antiquity and distinguishes between Chrism and Confirmation. He mentions that some believe that it is at this time that a guardian angel is assigned; he sees nothing incongruous in this, though,

---

[1] Canon Ollard, *Confirmation*, Vol. I, p. 154.   [2] *Works*, V, p. 658.

as we have seen, at an earlier date he had connected this with Baptism.

There is one rather significant statement which Taylor makes when he stresses that the gift of the Spirit comes through the hands of the bishop: 'I do not say that God is tied to this way; He cannot be tied but by Himself: and therefore Christ gave a special commission to Ananias to baptize and confirm St. Paul, and he gave the Spirit to Cornelius even before he was baptized, and he ordained St. Paul to be an apostle without the ministry of man. But this I say, that though God can make ministers extraordinary, yet men cannot, and they that go about to do so usurp the power of Christ, and snatch from His hand what He never intended to part with.'[1]

Taylor in claiming that these are exceptional people who had a particular dispensation begs the question. Might not a Fox, a Bunyan or a Wesley claim as distinct a call and commission from God as St Paul? Might not the examples he quotes point to the fact that, however valuable order may be, God is not to be confined to particular channels? To suggest that those who have been confirmed possess the Spirit in some special way that the unconfirmed do not may have been difficult to challenge three hundred years ago. The growth of the Free Churches with their record of saints and prophets makes the assertion more difficult to-day. The history of the Church would seem to show that God has been no more tied in the following eighteen centuries than He was in the first.

In discussing the age at which children should be confirmed, Taylor says that the practice in the Church of England and Ireland is 'that after infancy, but yet before they understand too much of sin, and when they can competently understand the fundamentals of religion, then it is good to bring them to be confirmed, that the Spirit of God may prevent their youthful sins, and Christ by His word and by His Spirit may enter and take possession at the

[1] *ibid.*, V, p. 650.

same time'.[1] If Confirmation has been neglected it can be taken at any age, even after people have received the Lord's Supper.

To persuade the clergy to make use of catechizing in order to train the young properly, Taylor equates the exorcists of the primitive Church with catechists. Professor Horton Davies has pointed out that Calvin favoured Confirmation because of the opportunity which it afforded to catechize adolescent members of the Church. He says: 'In this respect, whilst the Puritans did not use the rite of Confirmation, they preserved Calvin's intention by the thoroughness of their catechising and by their horror of ignorant or unworthy reception of the Lord's Supper.'[2]

The subject of Christian Initiation is one that is fraught with difficulty and there are searchings of heart on the subject in many Communions of the Christian Church to-day. The main conclusions of the Lambeth Conference Committee are worth repeating: '(i) that the gifts of the Spirit must never be separated in thought from Him as the Giver, Who is both Sovereign Lord and Creator Spirit; (ii) that the Spirit's activity is not limited to the Church, and that within the Church it is based upon the life and work of the Incarnate Lord; (iii) that while Confirmation came in the course of time to be closely associated with the gift of the Spirit, particularly, as in the West, it remained the Bishop's prerogative, yet "the dissociation of the Holy Spirit's operation from any part of the Initiation is strongly to be deprecated, as is also the attempt to measure His operation quantitatively"; (iv) that, nevertheless, the Holy Spirit's activity is conditioned by human capacity to respond.'[3] This suggests a rather wider view than Taylor's.

c. *Holy Communion*

The divergencies amongst Anglican theologians of the seventeenth century on the doctrine of the Eucharist is a

[1] *Works*, V, p. 663.   [2] *The Worship of the English Puritans*. p. 42.
[3] *Baptism Today*, p. 20.

study in itself. A rough and ready generalization would be to say that they rejected Transubstantiation and were inclined to Calvinistic rather than Lutheran or Zwinglian views, but apart from these agreements there were all kinds of variations.[1] Two main lines of interpretation were Virtualism and Receptionism. According to the former (which has been connected with Calvin) the faithful communicant receives together with the elements the virtue or power of the body and blood of Christ. Receptionism meant generally that the faithful communicant receives with the elements the true body and blood of Christ and more stress is laid upon the disposition of the communicant than in Virtualism.

It is difficult to know exactly in which group to place Taylor. There are passages from his works which could be cited to support either attitude, though in his later writings there is a greater stress upon the importance of worthy reception. This would be natural in view of his developing interest in holiness. Throughout all his writings there is the usual seventeenth-century emphasis of English theologians on not enquiring too closely into the mystery of how Christ is present, and Taylor is as firmly opposed as any to Roman doctrines. His position at the time that he wrote *The Great Exemplar* is summed up in one quotation: 'Let us love and adore the abyss of divine wisdom and goodness, and entertain the sacrament with just and holy receptions.'[2] Yet in the same book he suggests that the body which reigns in heaven is exposed upon the table of blessing: His body is broken once again and yet remains impassible: 'Every consecrated portion of bread and wine does exhibit Christ entirely to the faithful receiver; and yet Christ remains one, while He is wholly ministered in ten thousand portions.'[3] Taylor later modified this view.

[1] The subject has been fully explored in such works as C. W. Dugmore, *Eucharistic Doctrine in England from Hooker to Waterland*, G. R. O. Addleshaw, *The High Church Tradition* and *The Evangelical Doctrine of Holy Communion*, (ed. A. J. Macdonald).

[2] *Works*, II, p. 640.   [3] *ibid.*, p. 640 f.

In *Holy Living* and *The Worthy Communicant* we find that the emphasis is placed on Christ as our high-priest representing the sacrifice in heaven for us: 'Now what Christ does in heaven, He hath commanded us to do on earth, that is, to represent His death, to commemorate this sacrifice . . . the holy table being a copy of the celestial altar, and the eternal sacrifice of the lamb slain from the beginning of the world being always the same; it bleeds no more after the finishing of it on the cross; but it is wonderfully represented in heaven, and graciously represented here; by Christ's action there, by His commandment here.'[1] In linking the Eucharist with the Resurrection Taylor differs from the general attitude of his contemporaries.

Mr Dugmore has demonstrated that Taylor was influenced by Nicholson in his attitude to Holy Communion.[2] With this influence was combined his growing concern about Christian spirituality. We see traces of this in *Holy Living* and it becomes even more prominent in *The Real Presence*. There is a greater stress than heretofore on worthy reception. In the latter work Calvin is quoted with approval ('In the supper Christ Jesus, viz., His body and blood, is truly given under the signs of bread and wine'), and Taylor emphasizes that the wicked receive only the bare symbols while those who communicate worthily 'do by faith receive Christ really, effectively to all purposes of His passion'.

It is in *The Real Presence* that we find Taylor's sharpest criticisms of the Roman doctrine of Transubstantiation as being against Scripture, reason, sense and tradition. He joins issue with them over their interpretation of John 6 and declares that it does not refer as his opponents claim to the Eucharist. He believes that Roman theologians have themselves refuted this sacramental interpretation in order to reject non-Roman arguments for communion in two kinds. Further, if the words: 'Unless ye eat of the Son of Man and

---

[1] *Works*, VIII, p. 37 f. cp. III, p. 214 f.
[2] C. W. Dugmore, *Eucharistic Doctrine in England from Hooker to Waterland*, p. 95 f.

drink His blood, ye have no life in you' referred to the Communion, it would be necessary to give the sacrament to infants and no one who had not received the sacrament could be saved. The text, unlike Roman teaching, makes no provision for desire. Again, its spiritual meaning must be obvious, since some who partake do not have eternal life; because of their sin they receive it to their damnation.

In the light of the foregoing it is strange to find in Taylor's treatise on Confirmation that he quotes the very verse he has refused to take literally in *The Real Presence*. It is true that he includes a safeguard in commenting on the particular verse referred to, which allowed intention to suffice when the external means of obtaining the sacrament were not possible.[1] In *The Real Presence* he is less accommodating: 'This distinction (between desire and act) is made to serve ends . . . . Whosoever can be excused from the actual susception of a sacrament, can also in an equal necessity be excused from the desire; and no man can be tied to an absolute, irrespective desire of that which cannot be had: and if it can, the desire alone will not serve the turn.'[2]

Just as Taylor produced an Order of Baptism, so in his Collection of Offices is to be found 'An Office of Order for the Administration of the Holy Sacrament of the Lord's Supper'. He makes it clear in his preface that he has made use of ancient liturgies. Two examples may be cited from the Liturgy of St James: the opening prayer of the Communion which is a prayer for the preparation of the priest and the congregation; the prayer of consecration, which includes also a plea for the Holy Spirit to come down upon the hearts of the worshippers not found in the original liturgy.[3] Instead of including the Commandments as was done in the 1662 Prayer Book, Taylor uses the Beatitudes. More than once he refers to the sanctifying of the oblation by the Holy Spirit. This is in line with the argument in *The*

---

[1] *Works*, V, p. 628. [2] *ibid.*, VI, p. 27.
[3] *ibid.*, VIII, p. 616 f. cp. The Liturgies of St Mark, St James, etc. (Neale and Litterdale trans.), p. 44. There is a translation of the opening Communion prayer in verse form in *Songs of Praise*, No. 147 (1925 ed.) by G. Moultrie.

Real Presence that the Romans were wrong in regarding the consecration of the elements as taking place when the priest said: 'hoc est corpus meum.' Taylor takes the view of the Eastern Church that the consecration is made through the prayers of the minister and that the central act is the blessing of the elements.

Limitations of space prevent any attempt through further quotation to present the comprehensive beauty of Taylor's Order. We cannot do better than cite the judgement of Mr Ross Williamson: 'But Taylor was at least as good a stylist as Cranmer and a better liturgiologist and there are few to-day who, studying his Order for Holy Communion, would not find it an improvement on the Prayer Book rite.'[1]

[1] H. Ross Williamson, *Jeremy Taylor*, p. 103.

Chapter Three

TAYLOR'S PIETY — GENERAL PRINCIPLES

❖❖❖

From what we have already seen of Taylor's writings it can be assumed that he was quite prepared to wear the mantle of Bunyan's Valiant-for-Truth; yet it is probable that he felt more at home as Interpreter. The passing years brought an increasing concern about holiness and its achievement. Had he been able to look at our age he would no doubt have lamented our general lack of consecutive teaching and detailed guidance. If Taylor gives the impression of erring in the other direction, there is perhaps reason enough in the superficial attitude adopted by many in his own day. It is sometimes easier to die for principles than to live by them; the seventeenth century provides examples of both.

Moral Theology has been defined as the least which may be demanded of the Christian in given circumstances, and thus it has been separated from Ascetic Theology which deals with spiritual discipline and Christian Ethics which is concerned with conduct.[1] In spite of the dangers of oversimplification, the definition of T. A. Lacey seems more suitable: 'Moral Theology is concerned with the ultimate perfection of human life in eternal beatitude according to the will of God. What hinders this achievement is the particular kind of evil which is specifically sin. Moral Theology is therefore, on the positive side, a doctrine of holiness, on the negative side a doctrine of sin.'[2] With this definition Taylor would certainly have agreed.

---

[1] See K. E. Kirk, *Some Principles of Moral Theology*, p. xi f. (1954 edition) and *The Study of Theology* (1939), p. 363.
[2] *Essays in Positive Theology*, p. 121.

It may be asked why the detailed guidance included in Moral Theology seems to have fallen into decay amongst Protestants in the last three centuries. There are doubtless many reasons; four are worth mentioning here. There has grown up a healthy dislike of anything savouring of legalism in religion. The emphasis of the Pharisees on outward observance and the stigma attached to the word casuistry since the seventeenth century have combined to suggest that detailed guidance may turn the gospel into a 'nova lex', with the possibility of evasion on the one hand and, on the other, an unattractive rigorism. It ought to be remembered, in the second place, that the eighteenth century was an age when men were inclined either to the arid deserts of Deism or to the more tropical climate of the Evangelical Revival, where the warmed heart took priority over the enlightened mind. Neither clime was conducive to the growth of Moral Theology. A third reason has been the rise of Naturalism. This doctrine, though it contains some valuable elements, has affected the Church no less than the educational world. Put baldly, it suggests that, given the right environment, personality will best mature without guidance from others; the individual should be left free to develop what is inherent in him. Conscience, it is said, is a sufficient guide for man, and to-day conscience is frequently regarded as synonymous with common-sense. Fourthly, there has been a decline in authority. The problem of how much freedom the individual may be allowed in society is always with us. The Christian Church teaches man's responsibility as a member of the Body of Christ, while emphasizing his value as a person in the sight of God. How are the two to be reconciled? In finding the answer to this question to-day, men and women are less inclined than ever to hand over the keeping of their consciences to the Church.

It must be admitted that a healthy emphasis on the development of Christian character, through worship and the love of God and one's neighbour, may seem for the normal Christian the more excellent way. Taylor himself recognizes this in his introduction to *Ductor Dubitantium*. 'Preachers may retrench infinite numbers of cases of conscience if they will more earnestly preach and exhort to simplicity and love; for the want of these is the great multiplier of cases.'[1] Those who have been brought up in Christian homes, in touch throughout their lives with the worship and instruction of the Church, may find that they have clear principles on which to base their actions. Even so there are many problems which are hard to resolve. The Church does not speak with a united voice on pacifism, total abstinence, the remarriage of divorced persons or birth control — to name a few examples. The command to 'love and do as you like' may be suitable for the mature instructed Christian but, for the majority, freedom of this sort may well mean bondage to prejudice, pride or passion. The present generation is not one that is well-informed about Christian ethical standards; some have not realized the implications of the Faith in terms of character and conduct. Men are more inclined to a Laodicaean type of piety than to a scrupulous rigorism.

The beginnings of Taylor's interest in Moral Theology may be seen in *Holy Living;* his ideas are taken a step further in *Unum Necessarium* and are given their fullest expression, at least so far as the principles are concerned, in *Ductor Dubitantium*. In the first of these Taylor states that in view of the times which prohibit men from getting the help they need from personal guides, he has reason 'to draw into one body those advices, which the several necessities of many men must use at some time or other, and many of them daily'.[2] In the second, he laments the absence of books of cases of conscience; he is appalled at the easy way in which men live at a low spiritual level and still call themselves Christians. Before he can proceed to the question of conscience he must deal with the meaning of repentance.[3] In the third, he studies the principles in some detail: 'Moral theology is a collective body of all wisdom, whereof some things are demonstrable and many are probable, and other things are better than

[1] *Works*, IX, p. xxi.   [2] *ibid.*, III, p. 2.   [3] *ibid.*, VII, p. 7 ff.

their contraries; and they are to be proved accordingly, every thing in its proportion and capacity.'[1]

Unfortunately, this last work which was intended to set out principles became overloaded with particular illustrations; a hundred questions are 'solemnly handled and under distinct titles', while the number 'more briefly handled' reaches eighty. In consequence it has never attracted the general reader. Taylor's erudite contribution went off 'not with a bang but a whimper'. Yet the 1,300 closely printed pages remain a monument to his great patience, wide reading and deep learning, and to the thoroughness with which he worked out the achievement of good and the avoidance of evil.

Ductor Dubitantium is divided into four books. The first is concerned with the formal cause of good and evil which rests on whether actions are performed with the approval or disapproval of man's conscience. In the second and third books Taylor deals with the material cause of good and evil which is derived from the laws of God and man. In the fourth book he discusses the final causes of human actions or the motives from which men act. In this section we shall look first at Law and some of its derivative principles. Next we shall turn to Conscience and questions of conscientious doubt. This must be followed by an examination of what Taylor has to say in his fourth book on the will and the effect upon it of ignorance and fear, as well as the place of motive. We shall conclude this section with a subject intimately bound up with Taylor's principles of piety, that of Sin and Repentance.

Taylor uses categories which he borrowed from mediaeval Catholicism though he did not by any means accept all its ideas. Some of his assumptions would be disputed to-day; nevertheless, the principles which he sets forth are still relevant and we cannot understand Taylor's position without considering them. It is interesting to note that there is to-day a renewed and increasing interest in Moral Theology amongst Protestants, and Taylor's work in this field has received

[1] *Works*, IX, p. xiv.

well-merited recognition.[1] The writer is well aware that trying to reduce all that Taylor has to say to reasonable limits is almost bound to involve over-simplification of a subject which bristles with technical difficulties.

I. LAW

The general principles of Aquinas with regard to Law were taken over by Hooker who was followed in this respect by other Anglicans. These principles are well known and need only brief restatement. The Thomist theory started from the idea that Law is a dictate of the practical reason. Since God is Divine Reason and the Ruler of the universe, His will and purpose are made known in Eternal Law from which all other kinds of law derive. Natural Law is followed, we might say, instinctively by animals but rationally by men. From Natural Law springs Human Positive Law from which men develop rules about behaviour. The inadequacy of man and of the Human Positive Law led to the revelation of God of Divine Law which was revealed first in the Old Testament and then in the New.

While Taylor followed Aquinas in his terms, he was more critical of him than either Hooker or Sanderson. He defines the Law of Nature as 'the universal law of the world, or the law of mankind, concerning common necessities to which we are inclined by nature, invited by consent, prompted by reason, but is bound upon us only by the commands of God.'[2] He deals with each clause separately, carefully distinguishing between *jus naturae* (what is naturally right) and *lex naturae*, that which is imposed by law and custom. Taylor sees the weakness in making distinctions between man and beast and is critical of the consent of nations. Reason, which he might be supposed to admit as a valid authority, is marked out for censure too: 'Reason is such a box of quicksilver that it abides

[1] T. Wood, *English Casuistical Divinity during the Seventeenth Century;* H. R. McAdoo, *The Structure of Caroline Moral Theology.*
[2] *Works,* IX, p. 279.

no where; it dwells in no settled mansion; it is like a dove's neck, or a changeable taffata; it looks to me otherwise than to you who do not stand in the same light that I do.'[1] The law of nature to Taylor is ultimately 'nothing but the law of God given to mankind for the conservation of his nature and the promotion of his perfective end: a law of which a man sees a reason and feels a necessity. God is the lawgiver, practical reason or conscience is the record; but revelation and express declaring it was the first publication and emission of it, and till then it had not all the solemnities of law, though it was passed in the court, and decreed and recorded.'[2] This brings Taylor to his declaration that the perfect digest of the law of nature is to be found in Christ Who is our supreme authority.

The emphasis which Taylor places on the supremacy of the law of Christ leads him to examine at some length the adequacy of both the law of nature and the law of Moses.[3] The former, he claims, is obligatory only by the commands of God, while he points out the transitory nature of the latter. Both the ceremonial and the judicial laws of Moses are abrogated in Christ. An example of the first type is the Mosaic injunction to abstain from blood; of the second, the prohibition of marriage in certain degrees.

The Decalogue is not a proper digest of the law of nature, rather is it a tutor to lead us to Christ. In the sphere of love Christ's commands exceed those of Moses; Christians have a duty to acknowledge the lordship of Christ, to interpret the Decalogue in the light of Christ's teaching, to exceed the practice of the Jews, to go on to Christian and not Mosaic perfection, and yet they are not to expect justification on the grounds of conformity to the Decalogue. No Christian should regard it as sufficient to live according to what is usually called the law of nature; he is to live according to grace, 'which is reformed nature.'[4]

---

[1] *Works*, IX, p. 293.   [2] *ibid.*, p. 296.   [3] *ibid.*, pp. 350-495.
[4] *ibid.*, p. 408 f.

Throughout the discussion Taylor grapples with subjects which naturally spring to his mind as needing further explanation: whether it is lawful to have images, the Christian observance of the Sabbath, whether war is legitimate and how it should be conducted. How far are we to follow Old Testament precedents and how far the example of Christ? In making use of the Bible, Taylor says, for instance, that we are to follow examples where there is no rule. Examples are safe which have God's blessing upon them. We must go beyond what is lawful and discover what is fit to be done.

In dealing with the interpretation and obligation of the laws of Jesus Christ, Taylor again goes into great detail.[1] Much that he has to say would be considered rather obvious by the modern reader. No one would dispute that generally speaking a negative precept includes the affirmative; for example, 'Resist not evil' includes doing good to our enemies. Nor would there be, one would imagine, much argument about the necessity of fulfilling the spirit as well as the letter of the law. Taylor deals with such matters with the greatest thoroughness and devotes ten pages to a discussion of the subject: 'If the sense of the law be dubious, we are sometimes to expound it by liberty, sometimes by restraint.'[2] In the wealth of material Taylor provides there is nothing that is particularly new. It is of interest to notice the place accorded to Scripture as the supreme rule of faith and the very secondary place given to tradition and custom. There is, too, a strong plea against the extension of the Creeds: this, it will be remembered, is in line with his thesis in *The Liberty of Prophesying*.

The final section is quite short but provides a fitting conclusion. In moral duties which are common to Jews and Christians, in prayer and charity, in ecclesiastical laws and justice, in interior and exterior acts of virtue, the Christian is to show a greater measure of perfection. Taylor cites examples of piety from the Old Testament and pleads that

[1] *Works*, IX, pp. 496-704.   [2] *ibid.*, p. 548.

Christianity should produce individuals who excel in many graces as these saints did in one.

The emphasis which Taylor places on the authority of Christ at the expense of natural law and even the Old Testament is bound to attract criticism from those who feel that it leaves the non-Christian without any comprehension of the law of nature. Yet the events of the last fifty years, the rise of states which are entirely secular, the crude theory that law is the expression of power, the stress on sociological, psychological and anthropological considerations in estimating the development of law have led Christians to a closer examination of the Biblical doctrine of justice and law. While there is no attempt to deny the thesis of St Paul that the will of God is in some sense revealed to those without the law, it is recognized that even the Roman empire, for example, with its elaborate legal institutions could be a perverter of the law. The civil power has by Divine appointment the responsibility of preserving law and order, but the state itself needs to be redeemed and sanctified as much as humanity itself. The influence of Christians in the field of natural law may be a means to this end.

The Thomist position has been criticized in a modern Protestant statement. 'That method is to divide theology into a doctrine of nature and super-nature in such a way that each level of being remains relatively undisturbed, so far as its intrinsic character goes, by the other. Because law, as a phenomenon, falls within the natural order, its norm and character may, in principle, be known quite apart from grace, despite the darkening of man's intellectual capacities by the Fall.'[1] Though it would be a mistake to look to Taylor for a particular contribution in modern terms, we may note his stress on revelation rather than reason. This point is worth making again because Professor Horton Davies suggests that Taylor believes men to be naturally reasonable and noble.[2]

---

[1] H. H. Schrey, H Walz and W. A. Whitehouse, *The Biblical Doctrine of Justice and Law*, p. 119.

[2] *The Worship of the English Puritans*, p. 6 f.

Springing from Divine law is human law, and this is the next subject to which Taylor turns his attention. Though he lived in an age when freedom meant less than it does to-day, Taylor is prepared to examine closely the whole subject of how far human laws are binding and how far civil and ecclesiastical obedience may be demanded of the Christian. There are certain exceptions, he claims, to the necessity of obedience to human laws: if evil would result, if the laws are themselves unjust, if a law is founded on a false supposition, or if, in indifferent matters, the subject is outside the realm. On the other hand, with the exceptions noted, the subject is bound to conform with the law in private as well as in public, whether or not it has been accepted by the majority and whether or not it appears to be for the best.

Taylor brings his theories to a practical test regarding obedience to Christian magistrates. He declares that they may make penal laws and inflict the death penalty. He deals with crime and punishment at some length and the need of the guilty for repentance as well as acceptance of the sentence. The question of whether it is right for a guilty person to lie in his own defence provides one of the many examples in *Ductor Dubitantium* of Taylor turning aside to examine an explicit principle. Is it ever lawful to lie?[1] While Taylor quotes with approval the general opposition of the Bible to such a course, he gives as an example of an exception the borrowing of jewels from the Egyptians by the Hebrews. 'God', he says, 'gave them commandment so to spoil them.' Taylor is prepared to allow lying to children and madmen, for charitable and useful reasons, since they have no power of reasonable judgement. Within certain limits the doctor may lie to his patient and a besieged garrison may pretend great strength to deceive the enemy. Similarly it may be lawful to prevaricate to save life. But Taylor will not easily excuse lying and he applies the same principles to mental reservation and equivocation.

[1] *Works*, X, p. 101 ff.

E

In the next section Taylor turns to the subject of obedience to kings, another important derivative principle.[1] He states quite categorically: 'The supreme power in every republic is universal, absolute and unlimited.' This power lies in government not possession and it is for the exercise of right not wrong. Though in some sense the ruler may be superior to civil laws, he is not free from their obligation and he is 'not to consider the greatness of his power, but of his duty'.[2] Because his authority comes from God, the ruler is to accept the laws of God, nature and Christianity; as the people are his subject, so he is God's. He ought not, for example, to order his people to fight in an unjust cause and he must, both as king and individual, keep his promises. The royal prerogative may enable him sometimes to set aside the law; for example he may pardon a criminal who has been condemned. Subjects ought never to revolt against their king, and even an evil ruler should be tolerated.[3]

Taylor goes a stage further when he states that 'the supreme civil power is also supreme governor over all persons and in all causes ecclesiastical'.[4] It is with reluctance, he says, that he touches on this subject because he knows that it will raise opposition from both Romans and Presbyterians. He has little time for the arguments of either. Rome has proved herself to be unfit to govern the king, while the Presbyterians 'have not yet proved themselves to have received from Christ any power at all to govern in His church; and therefore much less by virtue of any such power to rule over kings'.[5] If kings are not governors in religion they are fulfilling only half of their function, since the offices of religion are half of the interest of mankind. Because religion is the great instrument of political happiness, surely the chief magistrate should be concerned about it.

Though the king may not persecute the religions of other nations nor the private opinions of individuals, at home he is entitled to prohibit new religions. Taylor is even prepared

---

[1] *Works*, X, p. 161 f.   [2] *ibid.*, p. 173.   [3] See also *ibid.*, II, p. 450.
[4] *ibid.*, X, p. 200.   [5] *ibid.*, p. 203.

to give the king supreme legislative power in the Church and he quotes with approval a statement of Gregory: 'Christ hath both given all things to the emperor, and a power of dominion not only over the soldiers, but even over the priests themselves.'[1] The supreme power may determine which doctrines are to be taught and Taylor mentions without criticism that English kings prohibited divines from discussing predestination: 'The public laws of a nation often declare who are and who are not heretics: and by an act of parliament in England they only are judged heretics who for such were condemned by the four general councils.'[2] The bishops need to make doctrines known but apart from the sanction of the ruler they do not have the force of law. If the prince errs, he says, it 'must serve the ends of peace, till by the doctrines of wiser ecclesiastics, the prince being better informed, can by truth serve it better'.[3] In matters of doctrine the prince needs the help of ecclesiastics, but he is not bound to execute their decrees.

The facet of Taylor's teaching that has just been outlined seems rather remote from our own day. While recognizing the reasons for the attitude which he adopted, the modern reader cannot help wondering what he would have made of the very different situation which exists in this age. He writes with wisdom of the dangers of entrusting temporal power to ecclesiastics, but his general attitude raises questions of some difficulty. These have had to be faced in countries where the civil power has sought to silence the voice of the Church or has tried to use it as a means for furthering its own sinister ends. Taylor would doubtless say that in such a case the Church should accept martyrdom; no doubt he regarded the government that deposed and executed Charles as being guilty of rebellion, and the fact that the old regime was established again might lend some support to his views. The modern situation is different and the line between antagonism, apathy, tolerance and active support on the part of the state is not always clearly marked. Had Taylor been

[1] *ibid.*, p. 248.   [2] *ibid.* p. 257.   [3] *ibid.*, p. 259.

alive in 1928, how would he have reacted to the rejection of the Revised Prayer Book by Parliament? Would he have been content to abide by the decision of the civil power?

Professor Wood has pointed out that 'of all the more eminent seventeenth-century English casuisists, Jeremy Taylor is the only one to write at great length about the peculiar powers and authority of the Church considered apart from its State connexions'.[1] To this subject we must now turn. Taylor regards the power of the Church, by which he means 'all the governors of the christian assemblies in the world' as purely spiritual and this power is expressed in canons and censures.[2] The Church has power to excommunicate but it affects only those who recognize its force. Since the Church has not met as a representative body for so long, Taylor believes that the bishops act as representatives of the Church and that their laws have a Divine authority. If these laws are confirmed by the civil power then they have a double authority and obligation. By the ties of religion, rulers are obliged to keep the laws of the Church, though Taylor insists that the ecclesiastical power may not excommunicate the civil power. In fact the prince ought to concur in ecclesiastical excommunications. Comment is hardly necessary.

With regard to the canons of the Church, those of the apostles have authority because they are accepted by the Churches.[3] Not all their injunctions are relevant to present needs, but the sacraments are of Divine institution and are to be observed. In things that are indifferent the Church is to use its liberty with caution. In this connection Taylor deals with the Lenten Fast at some length. It is not, he tells us, of apostolic commandment. It may have developed from a short fast which was kept before Easter, and this may be true of some of the other fasts.[4] Canons of the ancient general and provincial synods are laws to the conscience when the rulers of the Churches make them obligatory.

[1] *English Casuistical Divinity during the Seventeenth Century*, p. 87.
[2] *Works*, X, p. 275 ff.   [3] *ibid.*, p. 331 ff.   [4] *ibid.*, p 343 ff.

Taylor makes a particular contribution of his own on the value of Custom.[1] Those that the Catholic Church observes the Christian must accept. Baptism by one in holy orders is one example and the use of godfathers and godmothers is another; Taylor thinks that the arguments for the former are stronger than for the latter. He gives advice as to how far custom is to be qualified. In communicating with a Church with different customs, we are not to expect to make use of our own. Customs are to be judged by their present value; those contrary to ecclesiastical law can only be practised if the law is recognized to be out of date. Yet ancient customs, even if they are of unknown origin, are not to be set aside lightly.

Particular churches may make laws that bind their own members; they are to serve the ends of religion and do not have a binding force, even if they are taught as the laws of God. Ecclesiastical laws should be charitable and easy; they should promote the service of God and the good of souls: 'Ecclesiastical laws that encourage and adorn, and add degrees and moments and zeal to the service of God are good ministries of edification; and till by excess or accident they convert into evil, are of themselves fit to minister to religion.'[2] We see again the theme that runs through Taylor's writings that laws and rules are but a means to the end of holiness.

In writing of the ecclesiastical law of faith, Taylor realized that divisions in the Body of Christ make it impossible for the whole of the Church to meet together to discuss disputable matters of faith. The decrees of Councils may help but they have not final authority in matters of belief. When public Articles are established they can be useful for the unity and peace of the Christian community but, though we may subscribe to them, it would be unwise to swear always to be of the same mind. This would involve making the Articles infallible, 'or else a direct shutting our heart against all further clarity and manifestations of the truths of God.'[3]

[1] *ibid.*, p. 358 ff.   [2] *ibid.*, p. 411.   [3] *ibid.*, p. 447.

Taylor concludes the section with three points of interest. No one Church is to require with severity subscription to Articles which are not necessary, because good men who dissent will be afflicted or tempted to hypocrisy. If the ruler requires acceptance of the Articles for temporal reasons they must be complied with in such a way that the spiritual interests of souls and truth are secured. Wise and peaceable dissenters from the Articles are to be treated leniently. In such cases, the Articles are to be framed 'with as great a latitude of sense as they can; and so that subscriptions be made to the form of words, let the subscribers understand them in what sense they please which the truth of God will suffer, and the words be capable of'. Taylor adds: 'This is the last remedy, but it is the worst; it hath in it something of craft, but very little of ingenuity; and if it can serve the ends of peace, or of external charity, or of a fantastic concord, yet it cannot serve the ends of truth and holiness, and christian simplicity.'[1]

A brief reference must be made to Taylor's teaching about domestic laws.[2] He gives us reasons why children should respect and obey their parents. This duty is commanded by God because in some senses parents are in the place of God. There should be gratitude for their goodness; God has given them the power to bless or curse their offspring. Parents are to be reverenced in thought, word and action by observing their counsels, confiding in them and by being honest and truthful towards them. Natural law teaches this and civil law gives the father power to chastize his children and, in serious cases, to disinherit the incorrigible. Pity demands that children should support their parents in case of necessity. The power that the father possesses does not extend to religious matters. Taylor goes on to give detailed guidance about the power of the father in the case of injuries done to his children, of filial piety outlasting the death of the father and of the limitation of the father's authority. He is critical of those who have persuaded youths to enter monasteries

---

[1] *Works*, X, p. 450.   [2] *ibid.*, p. 451 ff.

against their father's consent, and he does not approve of children marrying against the wishes of their parents. The 'ifs' and 'buts' of the subject take up considerable space with copious illustrations. Taylor concludes the section by saying that the power of husbands over wives requires a separate volume which he hopes to write at some other time. Perhaps it is as well for Taylor's reputation with modern readers that this book was never written! We shall see elsewhere some of his teachings about the expression of Christianity in the home.

In approaching the question of the interpretation of human law, Taylor points out that even if the letter of the law is unjust its charity still binds. He is really pleading here for honesty of interpretation. The law-givers' interpretation is as binding as the law itself. Once the reason for the law is removed then it is no longer binding on the conscience of the subject.[1]

Taylor set out his teaching about the place of Law with great thoroughness as may be seen from this brief resumé. Some may feel that his emphasis is dangerous and mistaken. Ought we not to concentrate more on the ethic of love with all that flows from it? We must remind ourselves that this element is not lacking in Taylor, as we shall see, but that in this section he is dealing with that law and order which is part and parcel of every aspect of the life of man. Again, before passing too hasty a judgement ought we not to ask if there is not something in what he says that should be retained, or perhaps regained, by the Church to-day? The New Testament, no less than the Old, as Professor Dodd has pointed out forcefully, did not hesitate to stress the importance of the Law as well as the Gospel.[2] Lack of clear direction has sometimes led modern Christians to indefiniteness. No one would want the Church to be composed of those who have passed some rigorous examination in codes of behaviour, arbitrarily imposed, which might lead to a modern form of Pharisaism; but if we regard the Church as a school for those called to be saints, we ought to remember that every school has its

[1] *ibid.*, p. 501 ff.   [2] *Gospel and Law.*

standards and its code. If the Church is likened to a family the same principle applies; young children have to be trained and to learn that in the family as elsewhere there are certain 'dos' and 'don'ts'.

We may see the applications of this principle to the vexed question of the remarriage of divorced persons. Some of those who have been married in church have regarded this as a respectable rather than a religious action because it has been the fashionable thing to do. Has the Church made clear the obligations and implications of Christian marriage? Has guidance and instruction been given about the seriousness of divorce? If this had been done consistently there would be less reason for complaint if the Church refused to remarry divorced persons. In other words, it would be understood that Christians entering upon marriage accepted the law of the Church in this matter. This is only to touch the fringe of a complicated subject, but it does raise the question as to how far the Church has produced positive guidance for its members, apart from the condemnation of such obvious sins as theft, murder and adultery.

2. CONSCIENCE

This main section began with an examination of Taylor's teaching about Law, because it seemed appropriate to start with God's declaration of His will through Natural, Divine and Human Law before turning to its apprehension through Conscience. In following this pattern, which is a reversal of Taylor's, we are able incidentally to see that in dealing with Conscience Taylor has moved a stage further from the Thomist influence which is evident in his conception of Law. Criticism of Rome is more explicit.

In a valuable examination from the linguistic viewpoint, Mr C. A. Pierce has pointed out that in the New Testament 'conscience is the *subsequent* pain which indicates that sin has been committed by the man who suffers it'.[1] He shows that

[1] *Conscience in the New Testament*, p. 117.

later writers took over the more positive and objective ideas of conscience associated with the Latin word *conscientia* rather than the Green *syneidesis*. As a result, the Church today tends to regard conscience as a guide and the pain is suffered by the conscience itself. Taylor is in the tradition of the post New Testament writers. He follows Aquinas in much of his terminology and prefers him to the Franciscans in linking conscience with the cognitive rather than the conative aspect of man's nature, though modern psychologists in their opposition to the faculty conception of personality would doubtless criticize both parties.

Alongside the Thomist definition of conscience as 'the mind of man passing moral judgements', Taylor's may seem over-elaborate. 'Conscience is the mind of man governed by a rule, and measured by the proportions of good and evil, in order to practice; viz., to conduct all our relations, and all our intercourse between God, our neighbours, and ourselves: that is, in all moral actions.'[1] In developing his definition, Taylor declares that God reigns in the mind of a man in two ways: by faith and conscience. 'Faith tells us why, conscience tells us what we are to do. Faith is the measure of our persuasions, conscience is the measure of our actions. And as faith is a gift of God, so is conscience: that is, as the understanding of a man is taught by the Spirit of God in scripture, what to believe, how to distinguish truth from errors; so is the conscience instructed to distinguish good and evil, how to please God, how to do justice and charity to our neighbour, and how to treat ourselves; so that when the revelations of Christ and the commandments of God are fully recorded in our minds, then we are "perfectly instructed to every good work".'[2]

Conscience may be divided into two parts: *synteresis* and *syneidesis*. The former Taylor regards as the repository of practical principles and it may be trained and developed. The latter is the 'conjunction of the universal practical law with the particular moral action'. When the two are brought

[1] *Works*, IX, p. 3.   [2] *ibid.*, p. 8.

together they either acquit or condemn. He gives a syllogism to make his meaning clearer. What is unjust ought not to be done. Adultery is injurious and therefore ought not to be done. This principle is applied to the individual, and the act of adultery, contemplated or done, is judged by it. Taylor adds that though 'this is the proper and full sense of the word conscience according to art and proper acceptation, yet in scripture it is used indifferently for an act of conscience, or any of its parts'. To whatever aspects of conscience the name is applied the effect is 'that conscience is the guide of all our moral actions.'[1]

That there is need for guidance in training and directing the conscience, Taylor makes quite plain in his preface to *Ductor Dubitantium*. He, like the Puritan Ames, uses the illustration of the children of Israel going down to the forges of the Philistines 'to sharpen every man his share and his coulter, his axe and his mattock' to express the use made by Protestants of Roman casuistry. He says: 'We had swords and spears of our own, enough for defence, and more than enough for disputation: but in this more necessary part of the conduct of consciences we did receive our answers from abroad, till we found that our old needs were sometimes very ill supplied, and new necessities did every day arise.'[2] Taylor argues from a distinctly Anglican viewpoint which allows him to differ from both Romans and Reformers. As Dr McAdoo has pointed out and elaborated, the basis of Taylor's casuistry is Scripture, tradition and right reason as opposed to the Roman reliance on authorities, canon law and the confessional.

Casuistry and conscience are often linked together, so it is not out of place to look at this former word which has fallen into such disrepute amongst Protestants. Originally it was thought of as the application of moral principles to particular instances. Different schools of thought arose within the Roman Catholic Church, some more rigorous than others in what they permitted and commanded. *Tutiorism* led to

[1] *Works*, IX, p. 15.   [2] *ibid.*, p. v.

extreme rigorism and was suspect even before the Reformation. The Jesuists accepted *probabilism* which, in its simplest form, implies that if the lawfulness of an action is in doubt, it is reasonable to follow a probable opinion favouring liberty. This sometimes led to gross abuses and Taylor attacked it vigorously in his *Dissuasive from Popery*. He and his Protestant contemporaries settled for *probabiliorism* which implies that the benefit of the doubt is to be given only when there is more to be said against the validity of a law than in its favour. This system was abandoned because it was generally impracticable to give the detailed study required before making up one's mind. It was replaced by *probabilism* with certain safeguards against laxness. The late Bishop Kirk held that the belief of seventeenth-century casuists in *probabiliorism* may account to some extent for the decline of their influence and the abandonment of moral theology outside the Roman Church in the following century.[1]

This general introduction brings us to Taylor's specific teaching about the work of conscience. He declares its direct acts to be: to dictate and to testify, to loose and to bind. Included in these direct offices, but as reflex actions, are its accusation or excusing of the individual.[2] True peace of conscience is rest after enquiry, and it is as independent of outward circumstances as it is of the opinions of men. This peace is not experienced by the wicked for it is combined with a holy fear. 'Faith is the first mover in the understanding part, and the next is conscience, and they both purify the heart from false persuasions, and evil affections; and then they join to the production of love and of felicity.'[3]

Taylor makes a useful point when he warns us that it is possible to mistake for conscience such things as prejudice, passion, fancy, affection or illusion. Any unwillingness to look into details and a desire to look for the conclusion before the premises indicate that the conscience may well be misinformed: 'If appetite refuses to follow reason, and reason

---

[1] *Conscience and its Problems*, p. 260 ff.
[2] *Works*, IX, p. 16.   [3] *ibid.*, p. 35.

does not refuse to follow appetite, they have both of them taken incompetent courses, and shall perish together.'[1] The safest way to avoid error is to make an honest endeavour, wise enquiries, obtain the best help and pray to God.

The conscience of an evil man is a bad judge. The *synteresis* can be so overwhelmed that what is evil may be accepted as lawful. When the superior part is imperfect, the inferior (*syneidesis*) is an evil judge: such people 'sing in the fire, and go dancing to their graves, and sleep on till they be awakened in hell'.[2] In following conscience it is best to choose the truest, simplest and most useful interpretation. Taylor illustrates this principle from the subject of image worship. The commandment, he says, is plain; the sophistries of Rome obscure its meaning. The plain sense of the commandment is the best to follow: 'It is safer to walk upon plain ground, than with tricks and devices to dance upon the ropes.'[3] After this general introduction, Taylor goes into detail about the different kinds of conscience. He lists the tender, quiet, restless and perverse conscience but regards them as outside the scope of his enquiry. He turns rather to consider types of conscience under the headings: right, erroneous, probable, doubting and scrupulous.

'A right or sure conscience' Taylor defines as 'nothing but right reason reduced to practice, and conducting moral actions'.[4] General principles are going to be applied to particular cases, so it is important that the principles should be sound. 'Aquinas' says Taylor, 'blended Aristotle so with school divinity, that something of the purity was lost, while much of our religion was exacted and conducted by the rules of a mistaken philosophy.'[5] This is not to imply that Taylor was opposed to reason, but he makes it quite clear that the aid of the Holy Spirit is essential. Humility and piety help us to understand the secrets of the gospel because they remove the prejudices which blind reason. Conscience, therefore, is to be 'taught by God, conducted by reason, made operative

---

[1] *Works*, IX, p. 38.   [2] *ibid.*, p. 43.   [3] *ibid.*, p. 46.
[4] *ibid.*, p. 50.   [5] *ibid.*, p. 55.

by discourse, assisted by choice, instructed by laws and sober principles: and then it is right, and it may be sure'.[1]

Right motives are, of course, of great importance. Taylor illustrates this point by the example of attending church at Easter to avoid censure; this is to do a good act for a wrong reason. This leads him to ask whether it is ever right to try to persuade others with arguments that we find unconvincing.[2] It is legitimate to use arguments that we accept which do not commend themselves to all men. Scripture may be quoted and we may suit our reasons to the capacity of our hearers. We may also take advantage of the weaknesses, prejudices and false suppositions of the other party. He instances St Paul building an argument on the Corinthians' belief in baptism for the dead, though Taylor himself dismisses such a custom as foolish.[3]

There is a strain of sound common sense mixed with superstition in Taylor's reference to the use of fear. The question is posed as to whether preachers may for a good end create groundless fears: that liars will suffer deformity of face, that the devil in visible shape will haunt the perjurer or that leprosy will afflict the sacrilegious. His answer is that there is no greater evil than hell and the tortures of the damned. Curses may be denounced on the sacrilegious, oppressors of priests, widows and orphans, such as to die childless or to be afflicted with gout. But he urges that common sense is to be used. It is quite unreasonable in England to prophesy that a tiger will wound the profaner of the Sacrament. Fear may be used to teach children and fools but not if there is a good alternative.

Though the goodness or badness of an action is present quite apart from the judgement of reason (just as, says Taylor, an emerald is green before the eye perceives it so) yet conscience may make the object right or wrong to the individual. It would be possible in a doubtful matter for a man to change what appeared to be good to others into evil for himself. But conscience is always to be obeyed even if

[1] *ibid.*, p. 82.   [2] *ibid.*, p. 93 ff.   [3] *ibid.*, p. 98.

the man is misinformed: 'If a man enquires, whether he is to say his prayers kneeling, or whether he may do it standing, or lying or leaning: if his conscience be persuaded that he must do it kneeling, it is necessary he should do so, and he may not do it in his bed.'[1] In things indifferent it is not a serious matter, but it is always a sin to choose to act against the law of God.

Taylor comes next to 'the confident or erroneous conscience'. There are numerous causes of error which he carefully enumerates: ignorance, fear, morose humility, perplexity, irresolution, self-love, pride, prejudice and passion. Again Taylor urges that even if it errs the conscience ought to be obeyed. He finds it hard to excuse the erroneous conscience and, when he has dealt thoroughly with examples of what is and what is not allowable, he concludes that this guidance is of value in helping the man who is convinced of error. Guidance, as Taylor realizes, is not of much use to the person who is ignorant of his erroneous conscience.

If error springs from negligence or malice then there is no excuse for guilt. Taylor was probably thinking of the Dissenters when he wrote: 'He that makes assemblies against his prelate, and thinks he may lawfully do it, does an action for which by the laws he is punishable; but to God he is to answer besides the action, for the sin that led him to that error.'[2] Taylor almost personalizes conscience when he says that it is God's vice-gerent which makes His will known to the subject. But if the vice-gerent gives misinformation then conscience must answer for it. Yet, in the section following, once again Taylor stresses the duty of man to obey his conscience. He concedes that a man may refuse to fight for his prince if his conscience is so convinced but adds: 'He that is foolishly persuaded that all government is unlawful and anti-christian, is bound to lay his error down, and besides the vicious cause of his error, he sins in the evil effect of it, though his imperfect equivocal conscience calls on him to the contrary, yet he sins if he does not obey, because in such

[1] *Works*, IX, p. 123.   [2] *ibid*., p. 137.

notorious and evident propositions an error is not only malicious in the principle but voluntary all the way; and therefore may easily, and must certainly be laid aside in every period of determination.'[1] An act of will or opposite reasons may sometimes be of help, he says, in cases of error.

This brief summary of Taylor's teaching about the erroneous conscience shows at once both the strength and weakness of his position. He is unprepared to allow that reason is a sufficient guide because negligence or malice may distort it. On the other hand, there does not seem to be sufficient allowance made for the sincerely good man who differs. The history of the abolition of slavery is a case in point. Both before and after its abolition there were sincere Christians who felt that there was nothing wrong with such a system. It is easier for a later generation to condemn the blindness of the past than to consider where it may itself be short-sighted.

'The probable or thinking conscience' was a subject which opened up possibilities of a great deal of discussion. Taylor defines such a conscience as 'an imperfect assent to an uncertain proposition, in which one part is indeed clearly and fully chosen, but with an explicit or implicit notice that the contrary is also fairly eligible'.[2] Probable arguments may prevail when positive proof is lacking. Children, for instance, are content with reasons which differ from those demanded by older people. How are we to act when it is a question of two equally probable opinions? Taylor's answer is: 'That is more probable which hath fairer reasons, that is more safe which is further distant from a sin.' This may be a useful rule of thumb, but Taylor recognizes that there may be occasions when what is safe may contradict what is probable. 'It is safer to restore all gains of usury; but it is more probable that a man is not obliged to it. In which cases the advantage lies not on that side that is more probable, but on that which is more safe, as in these sentences that oblige to restitution.'[3]

[1] *ibid.*, p. 145.   [2] *ibid.*, p. 150.   [3] *ibid.*, p. 181.

It is not possible to list all of the subjects which Taylor considers and to follow him in his detailed guidance. We catch a glimpse of his underlying motives when he makes piety the supreme test: 'That which causes more honour to God, that which happily engages men in holy living, that which is the most charitable, and the most useful, that is to be preferred.'[1]

Taylor makes it clear that once the decision has been made it is not right to alter it for our own advantage. He gives one or two examples which may be cited to show how willing he was to go into detail and which demonstrate at the same time why the *Ductor Dubitantium* never became widely read. His first example concerns a priest who lived within the sound of two clocks, one of which was half-an-hour ahead of the other. The man broke his fast by taking the time from the earlier clock but chose the time of fasting before Communion from the later one. A master promised a friend that he would give him a servant and decided that it should be one named Taranta. But another servant, Ephodius, died, so the master withdrew his offer letting his friend assume that it was Ephodius whom he intended to part with. A man vows to fast and later decides to commute his fasting for alms. After breaking his fast he decides that he was wrong to change his vow. This decision in no way absolves him from almsgiving, says Taylor, any more than the master is discharged from giving away Taranta or the priest may juggle with the time.[2]

Great necessity or charity are the only reasons for doing an action when the probability of its rightness is slender. Taylor produces some complicated matrimonial problems to illustrate his principle. He is more realistic when he points out that in some decisions there is little time in which to choose. Then we may act in this way, for ignorance in such circumstances is involuntary. We need not follow Taylor in the detailed guidance he gives to the person who finds that his instructors are divided. He says that ancient writers are more venerable, though later writers are more knowing:

[1] *Works,* IX, p. 191.   [2] *ibid.,* p. 192 ff.

'They practised more and knew less, we know more and practise less; passion is for younger years, and for beginning of things, wisdom is by experience, and age, and progression.'[1]

Some of what Taylor has to say may find an answering echo in the mind of the modern reader; many choices that confront the Christian to-day seem to be between different shades of grey rather than between black and white. The complications of Taylor's principles for weighing up the pros and cons might be useful to a counsellor, but for the plain man would tend to obscure rather than clarify the issue. In pleading for a thoughtful decision, Taylor opened up the possibility of grave indecisiveness and of 'letting I dare not wait upon I would'.

Taylor deals with 'a doubtful conscience' more briefly. He says that it assents to neither side of the question and brings no direct obligation: it cannot therefore be called a positive and practical conscience. If a man is doubtful about an action, he may do it if there is an innocent or prudent argument in its favour. If the action involves someone else, then careful thought should be given before the decision is made. But though enquiry is proper if a matter of right or law is involved, there may be circumstances when it would not be wise. Taylor gives an extreme case. A party is out shooting with arrows and in the course of the sport someone is accidentally killed, though it is not certain who fired the fatal arrow. The man with 'an affrightened conscience' is unwise to enquire whether he was actually responsible; it is better to doubt than to despair.[2]

Taylor enters on controversial, if not dangerous, ground when he discusses whether it is lawful to suggest a lesser sin in order to prevent a greater. He asserts that it is wrong to take any direct part in sin, yet if a man is determined to satisfy his lust, it is better to direct him from a matron to a prostitute. This kind of example is quoted all too frequently; the number cited has been reduced to a minimum. Taylor is never really happy about permission to sin, and he makes

[1] *ibid.*, p. 205. [2] *ibid.*, p. 225.

F

it clear that no one is to use this argument for his own ends, but rather in the guidance of those whose standard of morality is low. They must be prevented from doing greater wrong. In some cases apparent evil may be done. He quotes Elijah causing a sacrifice to be made to Baal, David eating the shewbread, and Christians in China and Japan swearing by the false gods of those people. Men do not scruple to lie to save life, he says, and tell lies charitably to govern children. But Taylor warns his readers that men are too apt to seize on precedents and to make excuses. He concludes: 'A doubtful conscience is no guide of human actions, but a disease, and is to be cured by prayer and prudent advices, and the proper instruments of resolution and reasonable determinations.'[1]

Taylor has described four types of conscience and has illustrated what he means by each. Is it possible to make such a simple analysis? There are times when the man of good conscience must weigh up the probabilities, occasions when he is faced by doubt and sometimes he will act in error. Without detracting from the advice which Taylor gives under each head, is it not better to think of error, doubt and perplexity in connection with the problems of conscience rather than to picture the conscience as being erroneous, doubtful or probable? In other words, Taylor's approach might lead to a view of conscience that is static. He is really describing various aspects of the activity of conscience.

Taylor's fifth type — 'the scrupulous conscience' — may be regarded as an exception to what has just been stated, since it really describes a state of mind. To-day we should call its possessor introspective or over-conscientious. The sort of person that Taylor has in mind is the man who would starve himself lest he fell into the sin of gluttony or deprive himself of sleep lest he should be slothful. He depicts the scrupulous conscience in these terms: 'Scruple is a little stone in the foot, if you set it upon the ground it hurts you, if you hold it up you cannot go forward; it is a trouble when

[1] *Works*, IX, p. 262.

trouble is over, a doubt when doubts are resolved.'[1] It may be caused by sickness, melancholia, sleepless nights and undigested learning. He says that it occurs most frequently in women and 'monastic persons', in the sickly and the fearful. He likens it to a woman holding a frog or a chicken. Her friends assure her that it can do her no harm, and her own reason convinces her, yet she still screams. Spiritual guides are very necessary to help such people. Taylor says sensibly: 'Let a man look to his grounds when he begins to act, and when he hath acted, let him remember that he did his duty, and give God thanks.'[2] The scrupulous person should remind himself that he will be judged as a man and not as an angel. In general, his further advice may be summed up in the recommendation to such people to live simply and practically. Taylor was in advance of his age in finding some of the ills of introspection in physical causes, and in this he anticipated the conclusions of modern psychology.

Edmund Gosse in his life of Taylor assumes, perhaps too easily, that Taylor's cases are settled in modern times by common sense. Our own generation is in some ways as different from Gosse's as his was from Taylor's. In spite of the remoteness of some of his illustrations, Taylor laid down principles to guide those who were in need of ethical instruction. Our age, like Taylor's, is one in which many need such guidance, for life has become increasingly complex, and the common sense which Gosse thought sufficient against a background of Victorian and Edwardian stability is not really adequate for some of the moral problems which face men to-day.[3] Gosse remarks with some justice that Taylor's experience had proved to him how paramount a place is taken in the scruples of conscience by what Taylor calls 'odious things'. This results in illustrations that sound rather coarse to-day; they are not particularly edifying to read and cannot be reproduced. In this connection some words of Oliver Lawson Dick's may be quoted: 'In the seventeenth

[1] ibid., p. 263.   [2] ibid., p. 269.
[3] Jeremy Taylor (English Men of Letters, 1903 edition), p. 164 ff.

century sex had not yet been singled out as the sin par excellence, it was merely one among many failings, and Aubrey no more thought of concealing it, than he dreamt of avoiding the mention of gluttony and drunkenness.'[1] This statement applies with equal force to Taylor.

We cannot conclude our study of Taylor's principles of piety without some reference to what was the final section of *Ductor Dubitantium*. The law of God, in its various manifestations, which is apprehended by conscience needs for its fulfilment the obedience of the will. The will is important because man is, says Taylor, a creature midway between angel and beast; the mixture of good and evil is such that moral liberty of choice is agreeable to the whole purpose and design of human nature.[2] It is choice that makes virtue. For to deny that in the doing of good and evil there is freedom of the will would be to make nonsense of morality; to kill a man accidentally would be as heinous as committing murder. Physical and natural actions, such as growing and yawning are indifferent, but the same cannot be said of actions where the will is involved. However natural such actions as eating, drinking or talking may be, they are directed to certain ends. In this connection Taylor reminds us of the importance attached by our Lord to the 'idle words' we speak, for which we must give account. For this reason he urges a strict watch on our words and actions. Taylor answers the question as to whether good actions are to be positively determined and practised, by saying that 'He that is not against us is for us' may apply to those outside the evangelical covenant; for the Christian the converse is true. Either we are wholeheartedly for Christ or we are against Him.

We need not follow Taylor's remote and complicated illustrations to show how individuals may be implicated in crimes which they themselves did not commit, though we may note in passing that there is one question which raises a matter brought into prominence at the end of the last War in the trial of Nazis: 'Upon whom doth the greater proportion

---

[1] Aubrey's *Lives*, p. xix.   [2] *Works*, X, p. 550.

of guilt lie; upon him who commands a sin, or him that
sins in obedience?' This is but one example of the way in
which Taylor makes it clear that in the moral sphere man
must not seek to shelve responsibility.

Though Taylor traces the separate steps of volition which
lead to a sin being committed, he is quite definite that 'the internal act of the will and the external act of the man are but one
act . . . and whatsoever is done without is first consented to
within, and is but the ministry and execution of the sin within.
For the act of choosing is the foundation of all morality'.[1]

In his teaching about ignorance, Taylor follows the Schoolmen. In order to choose between good and evil there must
be knowledge: those unable to discern cannot be either
virtuous or vicious. Taylor will not concern himself with
such a subject as the attitude of the heathen who is ignorant
of the gospel, though he thinks that he may be less ignorant
of the ways of God than some suppose. On the other hand,
there are many Christians who know little of God and 'very
many for whom there is no course taken that they should
know Him: and what shall be the event of these things is
hard to tell. But it is very certain that without a man's own
fault, no man shall eternally perish.'[2] Yet Taylor believes
that men have enough of reason and of law within them to
know the will of God: 'Therefore no man can in the universal
lines and measures of salvation pretend ignorance: I am sure
we cannot, and that is all that concerns us.'[3] Ignorance about
God's law, so far from excusing us from our duty, is a sin in
itself. It is not possible, he says, to be ignorant of the existence
of God or of His nature, nor can a Christian fail to know
what the Church teaches as necessary to salvation. Though a
man is not to be blamed if he does not understand disputable
points, he cannot claim exemption from his particular duty.

Invincible ignorance is defined by Taylor as being innocent, either because we are not obliged to know or are unable
to know or still cannot know after enquiry. There are
obviously times when men think and act in good faith; though

[1] *ibid.*, p. 605.   [2] *ibid.*, p. 617.   [3] *ibid.*

they are mistaken, it is not possible to blame their lack of knowledge. But Taylor is not inclined to be too accommodating: some sins of ignorance are worse than some sins of malice.[1] Though he is prepared to agree that the ignorance of the insane is innocent and involuntary, the case of children is rather different: 'The sins of children are little, but they are sins.'[2] Because we do not know exactly when children reach an age of responsibility, we cannot be sure when God first begins to attach blame to them.

In some actions evil is a part of the action but in a secondary sense. 'Thus the boy that flung a stone at a bird, and hit his cruel step-mother whom he knew not to be there, said he did not then design it, but the stone was well thrown.'[3] Ignorance of this sort may excuse the action but it does not excuse the disposition of the individual. The worst kind of ignorance is that which is vincible and voluntary, either because of deliberate ignorance or choice. Taylor cites as examples those who put our Lord to death and St Paul before his conversion.

The question as to how far ignorance may excuse sin is one which raises difficulties. It is assumed, perhaps too easily to-day, that man is responsible only for known transgression of a known law. There is, however, as Taylor wisely points out, the responsibility which a man must bear for his ignorance. Taylor did not, of course, write from the standpoint of a psychologist who might lay stress on the influence of the unconscious and bring to light the ways in which so often we deceive ourselves. He does not state quite so explicitly as some theologians that man is a sinner as well as a person who commits sin, though elsewhere in his writings this emphasis is not lacking. Yet there are enough cautions in his treatment of ignorance to suggest that he was far from thinking that man could plead innocence on the basis of his lack of knowledge.[4]

---

[1] *Works*, IX, p. 624.   [2] *ibid.*, p. 628.   [3] *ibid.*, p. 629.
[4] A modern treatment of the subject is to be found in F. Greeves, *The Meaning of Sin*.

In discussing the influence of fear on choice, Taylor is not willing to make concessions easily. If I lead bandits to a man they wish to murder in order to save my own life, I am blameworthy because Christians are taught 'to despise poverty and pain and death, and to do all this cheerfully and gloriously'.[1] Contracts which have been made through fear are to be honoured. But while there are occasions when perhaps some excuse is to be found for failure, through the overwhelming of reason by fear, the same cannot be said for lust or anger. Such feelings do not attack reason as fear may do.

In writing about the important subject of motive, Taylor states that good actions done for evil purposes or bad acts performed for good ends are both blameworthy. He quotes St Paul: 'Whether ye eat or drink, and whatsoever ye do, do all to the glory of God.' This is the Christian's overruling motive. It is not right to serve God for any other end than Himself. To love Him is to abstain from sin, not because it will bring trouble, but because it is hateful. But Taylor does not exclude the idea of a reward: 'There was no love of God ever so abstracted by any command or expressed intention of God, as to lay aside all intuition of that reward; because in the receiving of that reward we are most united unto God, and shall in the best manner and measures glorify Him for ever.'[2] We must be sure that the end of our actions is all gold: 'If they be designed well they are likely to end well . . . for in the service of God a golden head shall never have the feet of clay.'[3]

This section on the will together with the influence of ignorance, fear and motive bears the influence of Scholastic teaching. But Taylor brings to his material his own distinctive stamp and, immersed as he sometimes seems to be in illustrations and allusions remote from ordinary life, his primary purpose is never lost sight of, as the last quotation indicates. And he is quite antagonistic to legalism in religion; the spirit must always be preferred to the letter.

[1] *Works*, X, p. 639.　　　[2] *ibid.*, p. 656 ff.　　　[3] *ibid.*, p. 659.

3. SIN AND REPENTANCE

We may begin this section by reminding ourselves of Lacey's definition of Moral Theology quoted earlier. It is on the positive side a doctrine of holiness, on the negative side a doctrine of sin. Our study of *Ductor Dubitantium* has shown how Taylor sets out his principles of Law and Conscience, through which man may discern the will of God. As a guide of frail humanity, he was only too well aware of the pitfalls of sin; as a physician of souls, after making the diagnosis he could prescribe the cure.

The stir that *Unum Necessarium* created about Taylor's attitude to Original Sin may obscure the importance that the author attached to the fact of sin, as distinct from its origin (which occupied a comparatively small part of the book) and the paramount need for repentance. It should be remembered that the whole title of the work is: *Unum Necessarium* or 'The Doctrine and Practice of Repentance. Describing the necessities and measures of a strict, a holy and a Christian life and rescued from popular errors'. To bear this in mind is to see Taylor's theme in its proper perspective.

That Taylor was appalled by the low standards of his age is made clear in the preface. In this connection he says: 'Men have found out so many devices and arts to cozen themselves, that they will rather admit any weak discourses and images of reason, than think it necessary to repent speedily, severely and effectively.'[1] In the second preface he goes further. The clergy themselves have neglected to take the subject seriously and some have entered the ministry thinking that it consists only in preaching sermons; guidance of the people in holy living has been neglected. Before he can produce his cases of conscience as a guide. Taylor is anxious to make clear to the many who do not realize it, the necessity of a holy life.[2]

He then gives the argument of one who might be an ordinary person of his own day who made a convenience of

---

[1] *Works*, VII, p. 3.   [2] *ibid.*, p. 8 ff.

religion. 'In the days of my youth I was frightened by the warnings of damnation, but there is confidence for me to pursue my own way in the religious books I read. I cannot help sinning, and I am told that I may be saved by grace. I am told I have liberty only to sin, and that though it is a sign of regeneration to struggle against it, I cannot hope to prevail. Yet God is merciful and though my righteousness is as a filthy rag, Christ's righteousness is what I shall be justified by, I am one of those for whom Christ died. It is not a good life which justifies a man before God but it is faith in the special promises. I avoid gross sins; I sin like a gentleman not a thief. Though I sin, I repent speedily, and my sins and repentances succeed each other like day and night. I am in a state of grace and if I begin to fall out of it I have only to begin to turn to find God ready to meet me. He has established a ministry in His Church to absolve all penitents; I have only to confess to be assured of pardon. Even if I repent on my death bed I shall be accepted.'[1] It will be seen that Taylor is describing what he feels to be the misinterpretations of various schools of thought, but it is done with the intention of undermining the foundation of those who built the hopes of men on words, and neglected the necessity for a change of life. 'By their fruits ye shall know them' might be said to be his watchword.

As we shall see, Taylor has no doubts about God's grace being necessary for our salvation, he is not one who feels confession to be without value; it is the abuse of these things to which he objects. Of himself he says: 'I hope I have received many of the mercies of a repenting sinner, and I have felt the turnings and varieties of spiritual entercourses; and I have often observed the advantages in ministering to others, and am most confident that the greatest benefits of our office may with best effect be communicated to souls in personal and particular ministrations.'[2]

[1] This is a summary of a long passage of Taylor's: *Works*, VII, p. 10 ff.
[2] *ibid.*, p. 17.

After these preliminaries Taylor settles down to deal closely with his subject. He begins with 'The foundation and necessity of repentance'. The first covenant which God made was a covenant of works, but man failed to keep it and consequently was lost. The passing of time brought with it new duties, and the covenant in consequence became harder. The law of Moses included sacrifice for small sins, but 'every great sin brought death infallibly.'[1] Nevertheless, this covenant had a place and purpose; it brought man to realize his need. To meet it God provided the new covenant of mercy. Even before Christ came, 'men were saved then as now, they were admitted to repentance, and justified by faith and the works of faith.'[2]

Taylor does not believe that man, who was incapable of obeying the law of Moses, will be able unaided to fulfil the higher demands of the gospel. He goes into some detail in describing the ways in which sin may conquer us, and points out that though different in form, temptation is as real to the saint as the sinner. There is a positive as well as a negative aspect in the righteousness of the gospel, for while the righteousness of the law consists in abstention from evil, that of the gospel includes obedience also to the positive commands of Christ. These new obligations bring with them (in the promises of the gospel) new abilities.[3] God imposes more than He actually requires in order to set a high standard, to encourage men to do their best, to enable them to grow in grace and so that He may give greater degrees of glory to those who excel: 'For as our duty is not limited, so neither are the degrees of glory.' In exacting these laws, 'Repentance was the measure of our duty, and the remedy for our evils; and the commandments were not impossible to him that might amend what was done amiss.'[4]

Taylor has no intention of proclaiming repentance as if it were a licence to continue to sin. He guards against this by his stress on the necessity for pressing on to perfection:

[1] *Works*, VII, p. 22.   [2] *ibid.*, p. 24.   [3] *ibid.*, p. 33.
[4] *ibid.*, p. 36.

'In this world we cannot arrive thither, but in this life we must always be going thither.'[1] He elaborates this point and says that regeneration is a state of perfection, even if it is a being made perfect by degrees. It is the perfection of men not of angels. Sincerity is the soul of it, endeavour is its body and 'the mercies of God accepting it in Christ, and assisting and promoting it by His spirit of grace, is the third part of its constitution, it is the spirit'.[2] Taylor gives advice as to how this doctrine is to be put into practice which is followed by a meditation and prayers. These are to be found at the conclusion of each chapter of *Unum Necessarium* and reveal Taylor's desire that the reader should apply the teachings to his own spiritual life.

In the second chapter Taylor discusses the meaning of repentance and examines the significance of the Greek words: *metameleia* and *metanoia*. He reminds us that both include a change of mind as well as sorrow and that they are used synonymously in the New Testament. Repentance is a turning from sin and a conversion to God.[3] The Latin equivalents *poenitentia* and *resipiscentia* mean the same thing, he says, and he criticizes the Romans who translate the former in the sense of doing penance. In this criticism Taylor is in line with his Protestant contemporaries. Repentance is leaving our sins and doing holy actions for the rest of our lives. This is conversion.[4] There is no antithesis in his mind between faith and repentance. They are distinguished by relations and respects not by substance and reality. In St Luke's Gospel the words are used synonymously, he says. Dives claims that if one comes from the dead that his brothers will repent; Abraham holds that even then they will not believe. Words such as reconciliation, renewing, a new creature, are other ways of describing the same experience: a new life in which we seek to please God.

Taylor then comes to the vexed question of mortal and venial sin. As is well known, there is evidence in the New

[1] *ibid.*, p. 37.   [2] *ibid.*, p. 44.   [3] *ibid.*, p. 62.
[4] *ibid.*, p. 65.

Testament for a distinction between sins. The Early Church distinguished between those that were scandalous (mortal) and others (venial) which were smaller in subject. Abailard was chiefly instrumental in changing the emphasis from the sin to the sinner in deciding on the gravity of wrong-doing. Though some sins were still classed as mortal, what had formerly been called venial could become mortal if committed deliberately 'with malice aforethought', as we should say. Venial sins were those committed because of infirmity or through sudden overwhelming of the will by surprise.

It is more usual to-day to distinguish these mortal and venial sins under the heading of formal and material. Though the sinner ought to have known, there is more reason for his failure in the latter case than the former. The late Bishop of Oxford pointed out that this distinction between sins may be dangerous for the sinner and from the Divine viewpoint is, of course, quite unreal. It may, however, be of help to the priest: mortal sin demands immediate and radical treatment, venial sin may be dealt with over a longer period.[1] By introducing the subjective element, the situation obviously becomes more complicated. Much must depend on the attitude of the spiritual guide to the motives of the sinner. May there not be a possibility that his attitude will lead to either laxity or rigorism? On the other hand, to try to put sin into two categories of deadly and not so deadly, without reference to the sinner, is bound to lead to unreality.

Taylor and his contemporary Protestants part company from the Romans over this distinction between mortal and venial. Taylor states quite categorically that to make differences is to hinder religion. He suggests that some Romans are more concerned about sin being mortal and venial than lawful or unlawful.[2] The Romans, he asserts, suggest that venial sins do not put us in danger of losing God's favour, and, since casuists differ as to which sins are venial, there can only be confusion. He goes further than his

[1] K. E. Kirk, *The Elements of Moral Theology*, p. 247.
[2] *Works*, VII, p. 83. See also *A Dissuasive from Popery*, VI, esp. p. 226 ff.

contemporaries in stressing the fact that sins can be greater
or less in principle as well as event. 'To rob a church is a
greater sin than to rob a thief.'[1] This is because more than
one sin is involved. In the example just quoted, both
sacrilege and theft are committed. Again, motive is important. To spit in the face of a priest in order to defy religion,
he says, is worse than killing him in one's own defence.[2] That
sins may differ in accordance with the obligation entailed,
Taylor does not deny, but every sin is a disobedience against
God. No one, therefore, is to indulge himself in the smallest
sin because it is equally antagonistic to God's will as the
greatest.

Taylor then takes up this supposed difference between
great and little sins. If sin is against the will of God it ought
not to be called little. To those who say that the commission
of venial sins is consistent with love for God, Taylor replies:
'The smallest sins are destructive of our friendship with
God.'[3] We are not to compare the judgement and pardon of
men with God's; God knows our hearts as men do not, and
we know quite plainly what our duty is to Him. God has
given us spiritual aids to prevent us from sinning. 'The issue
then is this; either we are forbidden to do a venial sin, or we
are not. If we are not forbidden, then it is as lawful to do a
venial sin as to marry, or eat flesh: if we are forbidden, then
every such action is directly against God's law, and consequently fineable at the will of the supreme Judge, and if He
please, punishable with a supreme anger.'[4]

The Romans, says Taylor, declare that a sin is venial
either because of the imperfection of the agent (as when a
sin is committed inadvertently, ignorantly, or by surprise)
or because of the smallness of the matter (stealing a farthing,
eating a little too greedily, sleeping too long) or venial in its
own kind (an idle word) which God cannot punish with the
highest punishment.[5] Under the first heading Taylor says
that any sins great or small may be made apt for pardon by

[1] *ibid* , p. 85.   [2] *ibid.*, p. 86.   [3] *ibid.*, p. 89.
[4] *ibid.*, p. 96.   [5] *ibid.*, p. 99 f.

the imperfection of the agent. They are in fact sins of infirmity and he proposes in due course to devote a special section to them.

In his objection to the second reason for calling sins venial, the smallness of the matter, Taylor says tersely: 'I know none such.[1] To steal a farthing from the widow who offered it in the Temple could not be a small thing. 'Every sin, even the smallest, is against charity, which is the end of the commandment.' Nor does Taylor show any more sympathy to the third reason, that sins are venial in their own nature. Though he has dealt with this argument already he returns to the charge again. God's view, he urges, as to what is large or small may well differ from ours. He concludes: 'No just person does or can indulge to himself the keeping of any sin whatsoever; for all sins are accounted of by God according to our affections, and if a man loves any, it becomes his poison. Every sin is damnable when it is chosen deliberately, either by express act or by interpretation; that is, when it is chosen regularly or frequently.'[2]

Though Taylor sees the danger of taking too severe an attitude, he fears the greater peril of Roman laxity. Wherever the line is drawn the remedy for sin of every kind is sufficient: 'Since these smaller sins are of the same nature, and the same guilt, and the same emnity against God, and consigned to the same evil portion that other sins are, they are to be washed off with the same repentance also as others. Christ's blood is the lavatory, and faith and repentance are the two hands that wash our souls white from the greatest and the least stains.'[3]

But how is a man to repent of his sins? In his next chapter Taylor comes to the question as it affects actual as opposed to habitual sin. Actual sin, he states, is an act of death but not a state of death. Therefore it is to be repented of immediately. He interprets 'All unrighteousness is sin, and there is a sin not unto death' as meaning that some sins are incidental to imperfect man, so that, providing there is repentance, sins in this category may be forgiven.

[1] *Works*, VII, p. 100.   [2] *ibid.*, p. 107.   [3] *ibid.*, p. 116.

There are three stages of grace. In the first it is possible to commit actual sins and even to have habits of sin, but he adds: '. . . but how long and how far, God only knows.' In the second stage a frequent falling into sin may be allowable, but if the Christian does not progress he will fall back into the first stage. Those who pass into the third stage sin seldom and repent speedily. Continuous growth is the only remedy against lapses.[1] Taylor's divisions are neat but they leave little room for variations in human nature. He seems to realize this in part for he raises the question of the good man who sins and dies before he is able to repent. Taylor hopes that his general attitude will be sufficient to overcome his single failure.

With regard to habitual sin, Taylor vigorously opposes Roman teaching which he says makes no demand for instant repentance and allows the sins of forty years to be washed off in less than forty minutes by an act of attrition and priestly absolution.[2] Though the rooting out of an evil habit is not a ground of forgiveness (as though salvation were by the merit of reformation), if God pardoned a sinner who still loved evil, He would justify him remaining in that state. God does promise pardon to the contrite, but is one act of contrition enough? 'A man's heart is not so easily broken: I mean broken from the love of sin, and its adherence to it.'[3] Contrition, he tells us, is not only sorrow but love for God and love expresses itself in obedience. Though Roman Catholics would no doubt say that Taylor had mistaken their meaning, there is no doubt that he was anxious that repentance should be something radical.

Taylor gives practical advice on how to repent when well, when old or when dying. The man who is vigorous is to be careful not to commit new sins. He is to avoid occasions of temptation and use bodily mortifications if necessary. 'He that is going to cure his habitual drunkenness, if he ever be overtaken again, let him for the first offence fast two days with bread and water; and the next time double his smart.'[4]

---

[1] *ibid.*, p. 138.   [2] *ibid.*, p. 178.   [3] *ibid.*, p. 194.
[4] *ibid.*, p. 213.

When milder courses will not prevail, let the penitent act severely; for instance, he can quit the service of the one who tempts him to drunkenness, or, if there has been habitual immorality, more violently still: 'Make thy face unpleasant, and tear off the charms from thy beauty, that thou mayest not be courted any more.'[1]

Though in general Taylor is opposed to death-bed repentances, he makes it clear that no one need despair who has time and ability to repent and holy desires. In what minute or degree of repentance a man's sins are pardoned, says Taylor, no one can tell: 'It is unreasonable to reprove a doctrine that infers a man to be uncertain where God hath given no certain notices or measures.'[2] Those who repent in old age are to remember that their sins will not be pardoned so easily as those of younger people whose passions are greater and whose reason is less. Let them draw their sins into a heap and spread them before their eyes in order to be ashamed at the number. Special zeal in doing right is necessary in order to make up for the evil which has been done. 'The old man that lived a vile life, but repents in time, though he stayed as long as he could, and much longer than he should, yet may live in hope, and die in peace and charity.'[3] Taylor closes with a quotation from Augustine: 'He shuts the gate of divine goodness against himself who thinks that God cannot or will not have mercy upon him, and therefore distrusts either His goodness or His almighti-ness.'[4] The other side of the case is put in a sermon preached on 'The invalidity of a late or death-bed repentance'. In it he says that the case of the Dying Thief is not like ours: 'When Christ dies once more for us, we may look for another such instance; not till then.'[5] And again, 'Let no christian man who hath covenanted with God to give Him the service of his life, think that God will be answered with the sighs and prayers of a dying man; for all that great obligation which lies upon us cannot be transacted in an instant. . . .'[6]

[1] *Works*, VII, p. 216.   [2] *ibid.*, p. 208 f.   [3] *ibid.*, p. 221.
[4] *ibid.*   [5] *ibid.*, IV, p. 406.   [6] *ibid.*

It is the Roman Catholic viewpoint particularly that Taylor is attacking in his attitude to death-bed repentances. In his preface to *Holy Dying* he says that God has made no covenant 'concerning sinners really under the arrest of death', and therefore he has none to give as the Romans claim to have. He asks: 'Can extreme unction at last cure what the holy sacrament of the eucharist all his life time could not do?'[1] The man who repents on his death-bed is only sorrowful because he is likely to perish: 'and such a sorrow may perfectly consist with as great an affection to sin as ever the man had in the highest caresses and invitation of his lust.'[2] There are similar references scattered throughout Taylor's works. If we miss the stress on God's willingness to receive any sinner whenever he comes in penitence and casts himself upon God, it is as well to remember the shrewd psychological soundness of what Taylor has to say. Is the man who has lived without God all his life likely to be sincere in his last moments? To deny that there have been genuine death-bed repentances would, of course, be foolish, but the number is unlikely to be large. As Dr McAdoo points out, 'The temptation to postpone repentance with the object of extracting the maximum from "the world" in the meantime, was very strong to the gay sparks of the day who still believed in a final reckoning.'[3] Taylor realized that men so easily believe what they want to about the results of repentance. They will repent but not restore; they will say that they regret, but rejoice in what they have gained; they ask God to forgive, but sooner forgive themselves, and suppose that God is of the same mind.[4] Taylor returns again and again to the necessity for repentance; he regards it as an integral part of the gospel.

True to his promise, Taylor comes to a full discussion of sins of infirmity. He begins by asking how far the unregenerate may go in the ways of piety and religion and replies that there is a middle state between the carnal and spiritual life.

---

[1] *ibid.*, III, p. 260 ff.
[2] *ibid.*, II, p. 377.
[3] *The Structure of Caroline Moral Theology*, p. 132.
[4] *ibid.*, VIII, p. 369.

G

Those in this state may be described as 'not far from the
Kingdom'. The moral but unregenerate man may be
instructed in the law and accept its authority; he may delight
in goodness and earnestly desire it and he may experience a
strife between flesh and spirit.[1] Taylor admits that the
regenerate man may do wrong, and it is difficult at times to
see where there is a clear line drawn between the unregenerate good man and the regenerate man who falls into sin.
We are bound to sympathize with Taylor's problem for
there are some who appear to fall into the category of being
morally righteous without the regenerate heart. It was to a
religious leader that our Lord gave the injunction to be born
anew, to a man who claimed that he had kept the accepted
rules that Jesus said: 'One thing thou lackest.' Those within
the Church as well as those outside it need to be reminded
that morality, like patriotism, is not enough.

Taylor believes that the regenerate man may sin through
surprise, ignorance, carelessness or through being asleep
when the enemy sows tares. Yet if he falls, he arises quickly
and fights more fiercely.[2] He tries to destroy the whole body
of sin. Habitual sinning must never be mistaken for infirmity.
Taylor defines these sins of infirmity as 'Such sins which in
the whole, and upon the matter, are unavoidable, and therefore excusable: such which can consist with the state of grace,
that is, such which have so much irregularity in them as to
be sins, and yet so much excuse and pity as that by the
covenant and mercies of the gospel they shall not be exacted
in the worst of punishments, or punished with eternal pains
because they cannot with the greatest moral diligence wholly
be avoided'.[3] Natural imperfections and evil inclinations,
provided that we do not delight in them, come within this
category. Sins of infirmity consist in failing to carry out our
duty rather than in the doing of wrong positively; though
evil actions which are done through surprise, fear or lack
of thought may be put into the same class. For example, a
wrong thought may come quite suddenly into our minds.

[1] *Works*, VII, p. 357 f.   [2] *ibid.*, p. 363 ff.   [3] *ibid.*, p. 373.

But sins of infirmity can only be attributed to small matters. It is possible, for instance, to have doubts about little things, but not about the goodness, truth or mercy of God. Taylor concludes by saying: 'The smallest instance, if it be observed, ceases to be a sin of infirmity; because by being observed, it loses its pretence and excuse, for then it is done upon the account of the will.'[1]

If Taylor is to be accused of severity in his analysis of sin, he did not leave matters there. An important section follows entitled: 'Of the effect of repentance, viz., remission of sins.' God's call to repentance, says Taylor, would be meaningless unless it implied pardon. The promise of mercy may be seen in the Old Testament, 'but when Christ came into the world, He opened the fountains of mercy, and broke down all the banks of restraint.'[2] He appointed an order of men who should exhort and restore men to repentance. 'All that believe and repent shall be pardoned, if they "go and sin no more".' Taylor adds an interesting explanation of the emphasis which he has placed on this pardon: 'I have been the longer in establishing and declaring the proper foundations of this article — upon which every one can declaim, but every one cannot believe it in the day of temptation — because I guess what an intolerable evil it is to despair of pardon, by having felt the trouble of some very great fears.'[3]

Since in infancy we neither need nor are able to repent, pardon could not be limited to sins committed before baptism. Some in the first centuries of Christianity, says Taylor, were too severe, and though pardon should not be promised too easily, there is evidence that true repentance brings forgiveness. Even if malicious sinners cannot be renewed to repentance by ordinary means (which is his interpretation of Hebrews 6: 4-6), there may still be hope for the man who repents of his impenitence. The Church cannot in this world pardon the man who sins against the Holy Spirit; this is a case which must be referred to God Himself. Some sins are pardoned without repentance: 'God

[1] *ibid.*, p. 380 f.   [2] *ibid.*, p. 391.   [3] *ibid.*, p. 392.

pities our sins of ignorance and winks at them.'[1] But some
wilful sinners are given over to a reprobate mind by God
because of their obstinate impenitence.

Taylor, for all his emphasis on the possibility of pardon,
makes it clear that relapsing into sin after repentance brings
great dangers. Therefore the convert must be positive in outlook and persevere in his duty. He ought not to be too
confident in claiming that his sin is pardoned. Taylor says
in this connection that some spiritual guides are to be blamed
for giving the sinner absolution at confession, and leaving him
to amend afterwards. This danger Taylor says is not so common
in the Church of England because so few make use of a spiritual
guide. Pardon is not to be judged by 'trifling significations,
but by long, lasting, and material events.'[2] After pointing out
that curiosity about assurance of pardon might lead to less
diligence, Taylor urges the anxious to consult spiritual guides.
We must seek to know ourselves, examine ourselves and do
our duty. If we do this we may leave the rest to God.

From the foregoing there is evidence to suggest that Taylor
regards repentance as a process. Both in *Unum Necessarium*
and elsewhere one gets the impression that man is on
probation. The sinner is discharged, but if he falls, his
previous sins may be brought up against him.[3] In one place
Taylor compares pardon with the incoming tide: as it comes
in by degrees, so does forgiveness. Alms and prayer bring it
further; such things as lust, idle talk and neglect of religion
make it retire.[4] Taylor's teaching about the doctrine of
assurance will seem to some to be lacking in definiteness.
While admitting this, it must be remembered that the
knowledge of God that a man possesses as he looks back over
his life must inevitably be different in kind from his assurance
about the future. There is evidence in Taylor's writings that
he could give help to those timid souls who were forever
fearful about the future, but there is no trace of encouragement to the presumptuous.[5]

---

[1] *Works*, VII, p. 413.   [2] *ibid.*, p. 419.   [3] *ibid.*, p. 417, cp. IV, p. 97.
[4] *ibid.*, IV, p. 98, cp. II, p. 546 ff.   [5] *ibid.*, VIII, p. 691, cp. III, p. 424 ff.

The last section of *Unum Necessarium* deals with the fruits of repentance.[1] These are sorrow for sin, confession and satisfaction. He defines the last named as opposing a contrary act of virtue to the precedent act of sin and punishing ourselves out of indignation for our folly. This is best done by those actions which demonstrate our love to God and our hatred of sin, such as prayer, almsgiving and forgiving injuries. There must be a deep penitential sorrow which is *odium* rather than *dolor*, a hatred of sin and its renouncement.

This question of sorrow leads Taylor to an examination of the meaning of attrition and contrition. The history of the words and the significance attached to them is complex, but it might be summarized by saying that when increasing importance was attached to the priestly absolution, sacramental confession tended to become more significant than the personal penitence of the sinner. This penitence could either be contrition, springing from filial fear (i.e. the will moved to repent by love of God) or attrition, arising from servile fear (i.e. the fear of evil consequences which could be rooted in selfishness). Aquinas recognized a midway state in which filial and servile fear might be blended and also a less worthy state in which a man might turn from God because of evil and the consequent punishment he feared. The Roman Catholics were divided after the Council of Trent. The Jesuits emphasized the importance of sacramental confession even if it was accompanied only by attrition. The Jansenists and the stricter Romans wanted contrition and sacramental confession. The Reformed Church insisted on contrition but were divided about the necessity for sacramental confession.[2]

Taylor himself thinks little of attrition which he regards as servile fear and as not possessing that element of hope and love to be found in contrition.[3] He points out that attrition is a word of the Schools not Scripture and that men make it

---

[1] *ibid.*, VII, p. 423 ff.
[2] See further K. E. Kirk, *Some Principles of Moral Theology*, p. 63 ff; T. Wood, *English Casuistical Divinity during the 17th Century*, p. 128 ff.
[3] *Works*, VII, p. 436.

mean what they will. He is quite critical of the Romans'
belief in its efficacy.[1] If absolution changes fear into love,
why did not St Peter give it to Simon Magus? If attrition
obtains forgiveness then it replaces contrition. For these and
other reasons Taylor regards it as foreign to the spirit of
Christ and His Church, a destroyer of the necessity for a holy
life and 'a desire only to advance the priest's office'.

A passing reference has been made to confession. We must
now see in greater detail how Taylor approaches this
important subject. In discussing the fruits of repentance,
Taylor, in criticizing the Roman demand for confession,
makes it clear that he regards confession to God as sufficient,
unless restitution to one's fellow is necessary.[2] He tells us
that the custom of private confession arose when the practice
of the Early Church in making notorious sinners confess
publicly dwindled away into private confession to a priest.
So, he says, this kind of confession is not necessary for
contrition.

To leave Taylor's teaching there would be to give a one-
sided impression for he values confession for other reasons.
For some Taylor regarded it almost as a necessity; it is of
such value to those who are 'heavy laden with their sins'
that to neglect it carelessly is a sign of not wishing for peace
of conscience. The clergy have been appointed by God as
spiritual physicians: their duty is to comfort, instruct, restore,
reconcile, advise and protect. They are able therefore to give
valuable help to the penitent. The self-centredness of the
sinner and the complexity of living as a Christian demand
that some expert guidance should be obtained. The minister
can help best if he knows the whole story. To confess our
shame is an additional restraint upon our actions.[3]

In his preface to *Unum Necessarium* the value of confession
is again stressed. Though there has been need to rescue men
from the bondage of the Roman confessional, it is not to be
exchanged for the tyranny of sin. 'There are some sins, and
some cases, and some persons, to whom an actual ministry

---

[1] *Works*, VII, p. 460 ff.   [2] *ibid.*, p. 438 ff.   [3] *ibid.*, p. 446 f.

and personal provision and conduct by the priest's office were better than food or physic.'[1] We may refer also to Taylor's *Holy Living*, where he speaks of the blessing of confession as 'laying open our wounds for cure'. He adds that we may be very much helped if we take in the assistance of a spiritual guide. To do so is to obtain 'the prayers of the holy man who God and the church have appointed solemnly to pray for us; and when he knows our needs, he can best minister comfort or reproof, oil or caustics . . . and the shame of opening such ulcers may restrain your forwardness to contract them'.[2]

One fact that stands out in these quotations is the use of medical language. This reveals Taylor as much nearer to the Celtic Church's conception of the confessional than the Roman. The latter was judicial, the former remedial. The Roman was concerned with the removal of guilt, the Celtic with effecting a cure.[3] The average Protestant (particularly the Nonconformist) is highly suspicious of confession and the vast majority of Anglicans no longer regard it as obligatory. To many it savours of Roman Catholicism (which is enough to condemn it out of hand!), priestcraft, absolution and a host of ideas which are anathema. It is regarded as an infringement of the liberty and privacy of the individual, even by some who would gladly lie for hours on the couch of a psychiatrist.

Whatever objections may be raised against some forms of the confessional, there is undoubtedly truth in the old adage that 'confession is good for the soul'. The positive side of confession, as Taylor understood it, would most certainly be of value. Clergy and ministers to-day of all Churches have tried to help those who have come with their difficulties, perplexities and failures, and they could tell of many who have found relief in doing so. Usually it is only those who have failed badly and consciously who avail themselves of

[1] *ibid.*, p. 15.   [2] *ibid.*, III, p. 208 f. See also IV, p. 590 ff.
[3] See further, O. D. Watkins, *The History of Penance* and C. S. Smyth, *The Genius of the Church of England.*

this means of grace. Were the practice accepted more commonly, there would undoubtedly be opportunities to prevent breakdowns later in life and to give positive help and guidance in the development of Christian character. Need this work be limited to the minister or clergyman? Some seventeen-century writers saw laymen too as the helpers of their fellows. One result of such confession or counselling might be to enable the person so helped to be a spiritual guide to others.

Taylor mentions that some of the Presbyterians examine some of their congregation before they admit them to the Sacrament. He says: 'It is no matter whether by these arts any sect or name be promoted; it is certain christian religion would, and that's the real interest of us all. . . . And there is no better way in the world to do this than by ministering to persons singly in the conduct in their repentance, which as it is the work of every man, so there are but few persons who need not the conduct of a spiritual guide in the beginnings and progressions of it.'[1] Alongside this quotation we may set one from Joseph Hall. 'The Romish laity makes either oracles or idols of their ghostly fathers; if we make cyphers of ours, I know not whether we be more injurious to them or ourselves. We go not about to rack your consciences to a forced and exquisite confession, under the pain of a no-remission; but we persuade you, for your own good, to be more intimate with, and less reserved from, those whom God hath set over you, for your direction, comfort and salvation.'[2]

[1] *Works*, VII, p. 16.   [2] *Resolutions and Decisions*, p. 455.

Chapter Four

TAYLOR'S PIETY—IN PRACTICE

❖—❖—❖

T he preceding chapter has been concerned with the
principles underlying Christian piety as Taylor interpreted them in terms of Law. His teaching about
conscience, sin and repentance may be included within this
word Law, if we regard it as representing the Divine scheme
for the fulfilment of the nature and destiny of man. We may,
however, look at piety from another viewpoint, since
Christianity is concerned with persons as well as principles.
The educational sphere provides a useful analogy. It is
possible to speak of education in terms of the standards,
curriculum and rules of a particular school. Yet the school
itself must express its educational principles in terms of the
pupil and his development, because persons as well as
principles are involved. So it is with religion. The principles
of piety have to be expressed by individuals who practise
Christianity in relationship with God and their fellows. The
Law is not abrogated, rather does love become the fulfilling
of the law. The Church has a duty to declare the will of God
as it is made known through Law and Conscience, to speak
of the sin which hinders obedience and to call men to
repentance. It has a corresponding responsibility to show its
members how they may grow in grace and, in communion
with God and man, be perfected in holiness.[1]

---

[1] In dividing Taylor's piety into principles and practice, it has been
impossible to avoid some overlapping. The life of the Christian in society,
for example, poses questions about his attitude to the state, and this has been
touched on in the section devoted to principles. Every attempt has been made
to avoid needless repetition, while preserving the sequence of Taylor's thought.

In attempting to set out the ways and means of living as a
Christian, we are confronted with the question of what is to
be our basis of study. It would be possible to choose either
the Beatitudes or 'the fruit of the Spirit' or St Paul's analysis
of love, and each scheme has something to commend it.
Happily Taylor comes to our aid, for in his *Holy Living* he
expounds the Apostolic injunction to 'live soberly, righteously and godly in this present world'. It will be seen that
the text produces three ready-made divisions: the Christian
as he is in himself — his standards of personal and private
conduct; the Christian in society — his behaviour in relationship to others in the state, the church, the home and business;
and the Christian's religious life — his spiritual development
through specifically religious acts. It is impossible to say
whether Taylor designed this deliberately or not, but his
explanation of the text provides also a commentary on the
seven Christian virtues. We shall in general follow Taylor's
scheme though the material used will not be confined
entirely to *Holy Living*.

In the first section we shall examine Taylor's account of
the Christian's religion. Here he comments on the Christian
virtues of faith, hope and love, and the religious acts by
which they are nourished and expressed. This covers his
treatment of the word 'godly'. The second section, concerned
with the word 'soberly', outlines Taylor's teaching about the
development of Christian character. Here we shall see how
the cardinal virtues of temperance and fortitude contribute
to the growth and maturity of the Christian. Though Taylor
did not include prudence with these two virtues, it may most
suitably be linked with them in this study. The third section
deals with the Christian in society. Here Taylor writes of
the virtue of justice. We shall widen the scope of his teaching
on the word 'righteously' to include human relationships of
many kinds.

This plan enables us to present Taylor's ideas in an orderly
way but it also raises difficulties. It is not possible in practice
to put these different aspects of the Christian life into

water-tight compartments; each may have an influence on
the other. Again, Taylor links faith with intellect, hope with
feeling and love with the will. There has been a tendency
recently to discard the old faculty psychology as being
inadequate to what we know of human personality. We may
stress one aspect when we say: 'I think so', 'I feel sorry' or
'I intend to act'; in actual practice the faculties are not
separated so easily. Cognition, affection and conation are
aspects of experience which include all three. Nevertheless,
the divisions which Taylor makes, both with regard to the
virtues and the faculties, are useful for the purposes of
analysis. They enable us to bring within comprehensive
limits much that he has to say about the practice of the
Christian faith.

I. THE CHRISTIAN'S RELIGION

We shall begin with the theological virtues of faith, hope
and love which Taylor associates with the word 'godly' in
his quotation from the Epistle to Titus. Though he recognizes that religion embraces the whole duty of man, including
the cardinal as well as the theological virtues, in the section
of *Holy Living* entitled 'Of Christian Religion', Taylor
deliberately narrows its meaning to that duty relating to the
interior life of the soul and certain derivative acts. 'Those I
call the internal actions of religion, in which the soul only is
employed, and ministers to God in the special actions of
faith, hope, and charity. Faith believes the revelations of
God, hope expects His promises, and charity loves His
excellencies and mercies. Faith gives our understanding to
God, hope gives up all the passions and affections to heaven
and heavenly things, and charity gives the will to the service
of God.'[1]

Taylor was aware of the difficulties involved in trying to
make this link both between the virtues and the elements of
personality. If, for purposes of analysis, we do so, there is

[1] *Works*, III, p. 145.

much to commend his association of faith with the intellect, hope with feeling and love with the will. Faith can only be exercised as the Word of God is apprehended by the mind of man; it may outstrip reason but is not contrary to it. Hope is linked with feeling because emotion and desire are involved in man's experience of God. The late Bishop Kirk has said that hope 'implies something much more than a placid expectation; it implies a keenness and passion exceeding that of any desire for ordinary things'.[1] Love is the mover of the will enabling intellect and emotion to find expression in purposive action. In the following pages we shall see how Taylor relates each to the interior life of the Christian.

In the New Testament, in the majority of cases where 'belief' or 'believing' is used, the intellectual element, even if it is present, is not the primary meaning; belief may be translated more suitably as trust in God. There are some exceptions, when the intellectual element is primary, and there was a tendency for this intellectual sense to become more important with the passing of time; faith came to be regarded more frequently as *the* faith. It has been said: 'About 50, he was of the Church who had received baptism and the Holy Spirit and called Jesus, Lord; about 180, he who acknowledged the rule of faith (Creed), the New Testament canon, and the authority of the bishops.'[2] There were no doubt many Christians in whom faith in both senses was strong. Athanasius argued and suffered for his belief in the Divinity of Christ; it was more than intellectual assent that enabled him to endure. The great phrase 'I believe in God the Father Almighty' has implied for some formal acceptance of the Theistic hypothesis; for others it has been the basis of the highest and noblest living.

As we know to-day, belief may be equated with credulity, superstition or the acceptance of scientific laws that have little or no bearing upon the quality of life we lead; it may also represent a philosophy of life which enables a man to

---

[1] K. E. Kirk, *Some Principles of Moral Theology*, p. 45.
[2] Heussi, *Kompendium der Kirchengeschichte*, p. 44.

die for his convictions. We have learnt in the past fifty years that in science as well as religion there is a place for 'artistic intuition' (to use a phrase once applied to the way in which Lord Rutherford made some of his scientific discoveries) and that probability in most things is indeed the guide of life; conviction rather than mathematical proof is what we live by. Nevertheless, no believer acting on the assurance of some internal or external authority thinks that his way of life is contrary to reason. Knowledge and experience may take a man part of the way; if faith takes him further, it is not a contradiction of what is known already. That would certainly be credulity.

A suitable analogy may be found in ordinary life. In the highest form of human relationship, a man and woman come to their marriage with a faith that goes beyond reason, though it is not contrary to it. Should a well-meaning friend try to dissuade the bride from marriage on the grounds that the bridegroom is unsuitable, she will doubtless produce arguments in his defence. Yet only experience can prove that her trust is justified. The act of faith which the Christian makes, if it goes beyond intellectual apprehension, does not absolve him from thought. There are some Christians who find difficulties in some clauses of the Creeds, owing perhaps to lack of knowledge; others accept them in faith believing that fuller knowledge and deeper experience will make their meaning clear.

Taylor has no doubt about the importance of the intellectual factor in faith. God's revelation is to be believed, and when we are convinced that He has spoken, we are to submit humbly, always remembering that there are some things beyond our understanding.[1] As he says elsewhere, 'Discourse and argument, the line of tradition and a never failing experience, the Spirit of God and the truth of miracles, the word of prophecy and the blood of martyrs, the excellency of the doctrine and the necessity of men, the riches of the promises and the wisdom of the revelations, the reasonableness

[1] *Works*, III, p. 145.

and sublimity, the concordance and the usefulness, of the articles, and their compliance with all the needs of man and the government of the commonwealths are like the strings and branches of the roots by which faith stands firm and unmoveable in the spirit and understanding of a man.'[1]

Important as the intellectual factor in faith may be, it is not the only one; the aspect of personal trust or committal is also evident in Taylor's writings. Faith is 'to give ourselves wholly up to Christ in heart and desire, to become disciples of His doctrine with choice (besides conviction)'.[2] Here both will and desire are included. We are to rely on God as we relied on our parents when we were children and should pray to Him without doubting. A combination of intellectual belief and trust is to be found in Taylor's list of the signs of faith. Not only are we to give up all our intellectual faculties, we are 'to be content with God for our judge, for our patron, for our Lord, for our friend; desiring God to be all in all to us, as we are in our understanding and affections wholly His'.[3]

If faith is viewed thus, it has relevance to the whole life and character. Assent to the Creeds without this personal committal leads to the formalism and hypocrisy which have been criticized by those outside the Church. Taylor is writing of faith in its fullest and deepest sense when he says: 'The faith of a Christian is his religion, that is, it is that whole conformity to the institution or discipline of Jesus Christ which distinguishes him from the believers of false religions.'[4] The importance of expressing faith practically is stressed when he states: 'Charity or a good life is so necessary an ingredient into the definition of a Christian's faith, that we have nothing else to distinguish it from the faith of devils; and we need no trial of our faith but the examination of our lives.'[5]

Linked with this idea of faith and its implications is the great subject of salvation by faith. Taylor was well aware of

---

[1] *Works*, III, p. 366.   [2] *ibid.*, p. 146.   [3] *ibid.*, p. 147.
[4] *ibid.*, II, p. 296.   [5] *ibid.*, p. 301.

the comfortable church-goer who was tempted to think of faith simply in terms of mental assent. His clearest teaching on the subject and its misinterpretations is to be found in a sermon on the text: 'You see then how by works a man is justified and not by faith only.'[1] Taylor objects to those who put St Paul and St James into opposite camps or regard them as leaders of rival factions: 'The one makes christian religion a lazy and unactive institution; and the other, a bold presumption on ourselves.'[2] Taylor reminds us of the different meanings attached in Scripture to words like faith, justification and imputation, and says that we too must be able to distinguish the differences. St Paul, he tells us, spoke of the futility of faith without love; 'If faith does not make you charitable and holy, talk no more of justification by it, for you shall never see the glorious face of God.'[3]

Three points emerge from Taylor's sermon. He believes that it is quite impossible to speak of forgiveness apart from repentance; pardon implies a changed attitude in the sinner. Secondly, however justification may be separated in thought from sanctification, in practice it is not possible to make a clear-cut distinction, since the former implies the latter. His third point is that the conditions of God's promises are binding: 'Let us take heed, when we magnify the free grace of God, we do not exclude the conditions which this free grace hath set upon us.'[4] Taylor reminds us that St James does not say that we are justified by works alone and not by faith: it is the 'obedience of faith', faith and works together. Faith is more than understanding, he declares, because St Peter urges us to add to faith both virtue and knowledge.

Taylor's conclusions may best be put in his own words: 'He that hath true justifying faith, believes the power of God to be above the powers of nature; the goodness of God above the merit and disposition of our persons, the bounty of God

[1] *James* 2: 24.
[2] *Works*, VIII, p. 284. He is referring, of course, to the doctrines, not the apostles.
[3] *ibid.*, VIII, p. 290.   [4] *ibid.*, VIII, p. 294.

above the excellency of our works, the truth of God above the contradictions of our weak arguings and fears, the love of God above our cold experience and ineffectual reason, and the necessities of doing good works above the faint excuses and ignorant pretences of disputing sinners. But want of faith makes us so generally wicked as we are, so often running to despair; so often baffled in our resolutions of a good life. But he whose faith makes him more than conqueror over these difficulties, to him Isaac shall be born even in his old age; the life of God shall be perfectly wrought in him, and by this faith, so operative, so strong, so lasting, so obedient, he shall be justified, and he shall be saved.'[1]

Taylor's *Holy Living* is concerned with the practice as well as the theory of religion; it is not surprising therefore to find that each section concludes with guidance about how to develop the virtue he is discussing. How is faith to be developed? One of the important qualities that is stressed by Taylor is humility. This frees the mind from prejudice. It is helpful too to contrast the wisdom of God with our own ignorance. That which is outside normal knowledge, the mysterious, should not be the subject of enquiry: 'No man carries his bed into his field to watch how his corn grows, but believes upon the general order of providence and nature; and at harvest finds himself not deceived.'[2] Taylor thinks that positive preparation should be made for times of temptation and weakness by strengthening our faith in periods of health. The great festivals of the Church may be of assistance to those who believe themselves, but are unable to prove or argue about the facts of the Christian religion. While we must defer to the last chapter a judgement on Taylor's attitude to salvation by faith, we may note that while he begins by linking faith to the intellect, it is not long before other aspects of personality are brought in.

Too often hope, like faith, has been misunderstood. It has not infrequently been equated with an unthinking optimism. Is it any wonder that it is the most neglected of the Christian

[1] *Works*, VIII, p. 302.   [2] *ibid.*, III, p. 149.

virtues, though want of hope leads to an escapist or fatalistic attitude? We may with Taylor link hope with feeling but, as with faith, we shall see that it cannot be confined to one facet of personality. Taylor agrees with St Augustine that faith is concerned with everything revealed, good and bad, past, present and to come, and with things which may or may not involve us; 'but hope hath for its object things only that are good, and fit to be hoped for, future, and concerning ourselves.'[1]

In one sense hope is less certain than faith, says Taylor, because its fulfilment depends upon our keeping the conditions of the promise. Amongst the acts of hope he lists are: reliance upon God, a confident expectation of His promises, a trust in His over-ruling providence even when things go wrong for us, 'rejoicing in tribulation', desiring, praying and longing for the great object of our hope. This virtue is of particular value in our prayers, which in proportion to our hope will be zealous and affectionate. Indeed, without it, it is impossible to pray. The perfection of hope is perseverance.[2] Hope is to be measured by our state and person with regard to gifts, graces and temporal favours, and it is to be concerned with what is possible and useful. The Christian should cherish it in his heart rather than talk a great deal about it.

Taylor knows that the great enemy of hope is despair. Here the mind may come to the aid of the emotions: 'Apply your mind to the cure of all the proper causes of despair.'[3] Weakness of spirit, violence of passion, covetousness and faint-heartedness may all be hindrances to hope. In material things, we may believe that in reasonable matters such as paying our debts, recovery from illness, deliverance from our enemies or shipwreck, Divine help will be forthcoming; there is Scriptural evidence for God's intervention in human affairs, and if we may trust Him in general then we may trust Him in particular. Even when death approaches, acceptance of it may bring freedom from

[1] *ibid.*, p. 150.   [2] *ibid.*, p. 151.   [3] *ibid.*, p. 152.

H

despair as we lose hope of living, 'for when you enter into
the regions of death, you rest from all your labours and
your fears.'[1]

In considering Taylor's teaching about repentance, we
noticed that he had something to say to those who despaired
of being pardoned. Since his attitude to the doctrine of
assurance seems to vary, it is worth while looking at the
subject again from the point of view of his practical advice
in *Holy Living*. Those who despair of salvation should remind
themselves of how much Christ has suffered to deliver us;
God's desire to save us therefore is infinite: 'As the hope of
salvation is a good disposition to it, so is despair a certain
consignment to eternal ruin. A man may be damned for
despairing to be saved.' To remember God's grace in the
past is of great help: 'For although the conjectures and
expectations of hope are not like the conclusions of faith, yet
they are a helmet against the scorchings of despair in
temporal things, and an anchor of the soul sure and steadfast
against the fluctuations of the spirit in matters of the
soul.'[2] Taylor was always afraid that men would become
presumptious. Bunyan's Christian who leaped for joy
when the burden fell off his back is not to be found in
the pages of Taylor's works. All his caution goes into the
phrase: 'The fearing man is safest.' But fearing to offend
does not exclude modest hopes, and this surely is better
than presumption.[3]

There is of course a direct link between hope and penitence, for both have an element of desire in them. This
emphasis is not so explicit in *Holy Living* as in *Unum Necessarium*. Taylor mentions it in the latter work in his teaching
about contrition, which he contrasts with attrition which has
no hope in it. It will be remembered that in *Unum Necessarium*
repentance and faith are represented as facets of the same
experience, and in it hope has its rightful and due place:
'This becoming His disciples is called faith, that is, coming
to Him, believing Him, hoping in Him, obeying Him; and

[1] *Works*, III, p. 154.   [2] *ibid.*, p. 154.   [3] See also *Works*, III, p. 424 ff.

consequent to this is, that we are admitted to repentance, that is, to pardon of our sins.'[1]

We have noticed already that faith and hope may be limited in definition and misunderstood; it is only too apparent to-day that the coinage of the word love has also been debased. Faith, hope and love are frequently equated with credulity, wishful thinking and sentimentality. To begin by associating love with the will, even if we recognize the limitations of so doing, at least delivers us from thinking of it simply in terms of feeling. Love, of course, is no more to be confined to purposive action than faith is to be limited to an intellectual concept or hope to be thought of simply in terms of desire; and as the facets of personality merge into one another, so may their connections with the virtues.

The link between love and the will is made clear by Taylor in his section on the acts of love to God. Love demands more than obedience, for we are to go beyond our duty. It implies cheerfully and willingly enduring all things, with an impatience of all that is contrary to God's will. Just as the lover seeks to be united to the beloved and cannot bear separation, so nothing can compensate the Christian for the absence of God: 'For we are not to use God and religion as men use perfumes, with which they are delighted when they have them, but can very well be without them.'[2] The lover of God chooses as He likes and is ruled by His judgement, desiring to learn where God is the teacher. He strives to avoid doing the smallest things which might offend Him.

It will be seen from the above that Taylor, even in his analogy of human love, gives prominence to the will. What then of emotion? He is so afraid that wrong desires may sully our love for God that he gives three rules of Divine love. Love is to be without violence and transportation, he says, and expressed in holy actions: 'A new beginner in religion hath passionate and violent desires; but they must not be the measure of his actions. . . . Indiscreet violences and

<hr>

[1] *ibid.*, VII, p. 66.   [2] *ibid.*, III, p. 158.

untimely forwardness are the rocks of religion, against which
tender spirits often suffer shipwreck.' Secondly, we are to
express our love prudently: 'We cannot love God too much,
but we may proclaim it in undecent manners.' Thirdly, love is
to be firm and constant, not like the ebb and flow of the tide. [1]

In order to develop this love for God we are to renounce
excessive affection for the things of this world, and, of course,
all desire for sin. We are to be careful what we allow to fill
our 'fancy'. as Taylor calls it. We should transplant the
instruments of fancy into religion: it is for this reason that
we have in churches music, ornaments, perfumes, comely
garments and decent ceremonies, 'that the busy and less
discerning fancy, being bribed with its proper objects, may
be instrumental to a more celestial and spiritual love'. [2] Too
great a preoccupation with the things of this life may hinder
our love: country, neighbours and tradesmen all demand
some care and attention, but these lesser responsibilities
should not detract from the love which is due to God. An
effort of will is necessary to make sure that we love God first,
and we should pray frequently to Him about every aspect
of life: 'Call to Him for health, run to Him for counsel, beg
of Him for pardon.' We may strengthen our love for God
by considering His love for us in creation, preservation,
redemption, forgiveness and adoption.

This brings Taylor to a consideration of the two states of
love to God. He says in this connection: 'The least love that
is, must be obedient, pure, simple and communicative: that
is, it must exclude all affection to sin, and all inordinate
affection to the world, and must be expressive, according to
our power, in the instances of duty, and must be love for
love's sake.' [3] The highest example of this love is martyrdom
which is a readiness to suffer rather than to do evil. Even the
most imperfect should have love of this quality and 'must
differ from another in nothing except in the degrees of
promptness and alacrity'. 'But', adds Taylor, 'the greater
state of love is the zeal of love, which runs out into

[1] *Works*, III, p. 158 f.   [2] *ibid.*, p. 160.   [3] *ibid.*, p. 161.

excrescences and suckers, like a fruitful and pleasant tree; or bursting into gums, and producing fruits, not of a monstrous, but of an extraordinary and heroical greatness.'[1]

It will have been noticed that Taylor's definition of love is severely practical, and that he is anxious to control the part that feeling plays. The fact that he is now passing to the zeal of love might in another writer mean that more prominence is to be given to emotion, for zeal is often equated with enthusiasm. But Taylor heads the section: 'Cautions and rules concerning zeal.' It is not to be confused, he says, with passion or forwardness. These produce, in some who have just begun the spiritual life, an enthusiasm which is transient. Whatever our feelings, zeal is to be expressed in moderation: 'For let affection boil as high as it can, yet if it boil over into irregular and strange actions, it will have but few, but will need many, excuses.' It is safer to apply our zeal to our duty rather than in 'too forward vows of chastity, and restraints of natural and innocent liberties'.[2] Care and restraint are necessary in the application of the zeal of love when others are involved.

In the direct actions of religion zeal may be unbounded: 'Do all the parts of your duty as earnestly as if the salvation of all the world, and the whole glory of God, and the confusion of all devils, and all that you hope or desire, did depend upon every one action.' Taylor's final point speaks for itself. 'Let zeal be seated in the will and choice, and regulated with prudence and a sober understanding, not in fancies and affections; for these will make it full of noise and empty of profit; but that will make it deep and smooth, material and devout.'[3] Elsewhere Taylor says that zeal is to be concerned with what is possible: 'He that vows never to have an ill thought, never to commit an error, hath taken a course that his little infirmities shall become crimes . . . .'[4]

This love for God will obviously manifest itself in obedience. 'If a man says his prayers or communicates, out of custom, or without intuition of the precept or divine

[1] *ibid.*, p. 161.   [2] *ibid.*, p. 162.   [3] *ibid.*, p. 163.
[4] *ibid.*, IV, p. 178.

commandment, the act is like a ship returning from her voyage without her venture and her burden, as unprofitable as without stowage. But if God commands us either to eat or to abstain, to sleep or to be waking, to work or to keep a sabbath, these actions, which are naturally neither good nor evil, are sanctified by the obedience, and ranked among actions of the greatest excellency.'[1] Obedience is not simply the outward act, 'but a sacrifice of our proper will to God, a choosing the duty because God commands it.' Beasts work by compulsion, slaves out of fear of their masters, but sons serve their fathers with love. To give gold to God is suitable for beginners in religion; mature Christians give Him their wills. This surrender of the will implies service which goes beyond the letter of the law. It involves too the yielding of our reason: 'From the composition of the will and affections with our exterior acts of obedience to God, our obedience is made willing, swift and cheerful; but from the composition of the understanding our obedience becomes strong, sincere and persevering; and this is that which St Paul calls "our reasonable service".'[2]

It is hoped that enough has been set out of Taylor's teaching about the place of faith, hope and love to show that while links with the cognitive, affective and conative aspects of experience may be made, there is difficulty from both sides in sustaining such divisions; they are really only convenient starting-points. Obviously the virtues themselves are capable of much more detailed study. The aim has been to sketch Taylor's general attitude for, without extending discussion, there is much that is thought-provoking, and to understand Taylor's implications could be enriching for many Church members. Perhaps his descriptions of the virtues are so qualified that we miss the spontaneous element in them that made Early Christianity contagious. Does he, on the other hand, bring a more serious spirit to his understanding of the Faith than is customary in much that passes for Christianity to-day?

[1] *Works*, II, p. 106.   [2] *ibid.*, p. 111.

Faith, hope and love, Taylor held, were to find expression in religious acts which in turn would aid the development of the virtues in the life of the Christian. These actions Taylor divides into internal and mixed. The former includes things which are done to God alone: reading and hearing the Word of God, fasting, the observance of the Lord's day and of festivals. The latter group is concerned with actions in which God and man may be involved: prayer, almsgiving, repentance and receiving the Sacrament.

Taylor defines God's Word as 'all those commandments and revelations, those promisings and threatenings, the stories and sermons recorded in the Bible; nothing else is the word of God that we know of by any certain instrument.'[1] Homilies, sermons and good books are no more than commentary on Scripture. Taylor, as we shall see later, gives due place to the sermon, so that we may regard as a kind of poetic licence his statement that the words of Scripture are the best sermons, as the Holy Spirit is the best teacher. In the Bible, he says, we have the way of salvation set down so that even the ignorant may understand his duty.

Taylor believes that time should be set apart for reading the Bible, and it is interesting to note that he advocates selection in reading. He mentions the Gospels, Psalms and the lessons appointed to be read on Sundays and holy days. A spiritual guide may help us in advising on the choice of spiritual books. To public reading of the Scriptures we should listen attentively, asking for God's illumination. We have already noticed Taylor's emphasis on the necessity for reason to be informed by the Spirit of God. Referring to the Holy Spirit, he says: 'He opens the heart, not to receive murmurs, or to attend to secret whispers, but to hear the word of God. . . . Without this, we may hear the word of God, but we can never understand it.'[2] Though learning has its uses, it needs to be inspired by God; Pythagoras and Plato were

---

[1] *ibid.*, III, p. 164. See also Taylor's emphasis on the sufficiency of Scripture for salvation in his *Dissuasive from Popery, Works*, VI, p. 380 ff.

[2] *ibid.*, VIII, p. 377.

students of Moses' books, says Taylor, but did not become Jews.

If Christians to-day see some point in Taylor's injunctions to study the Bible, there may be less agreement about the necessity to fast. It is not to be considered as a duty, says Taylor, unless there is a spiritual end.[1] He regards it as a useful means of subduing the flesh and removing hindrances. When it is connected with repentance it should be 'short, sharp and afflictive'. In such cases quality is more important than quantity; there should be a refusal of the more pleasant for the more wholesome. Fasting is to be linked with other external signs of repentance: 'For a man must not, when he mourns in his fast, be merry in his sport; weep at dinner and laugh all day after, have a silence in his kitchen and music in his chamber, judge the stomach and feast the other senses.' If fasting is connected with mortification, with the intention of subduing bodily desire, it must be more prolonged: 'A daily lessening our portion of meat and drink, and a choosing such a coarse diet which may make the least preparation for the lusts of the body.' While Taylor thinks that fasts ordained by lawful authority should be observed, he is careful to state that fasting is not to endanger health nor be imposed upon the sick, the aged, wearied travellers, women with child, children and the poor. It is to be compared with medicine, and has been called 'the nourishment of prayer, the restraint of lust, the wings of the soul, the diet of angels, the instrument of humility and self-denial, the purification of the spirit'.[2]

Apart from abstention from food before Holy Communion, commended by Taylor, and some self-denial in Lent, fasting is not generally observed by most Christians to-day. Two wars involving rationing have possibly contributed to its disappearance. Those who do fast, it must be admitted, are more likely to do it for reasons of the body than the soul! Taylor is right in setting the subject in the context of a

[1] *Works*, III, p. 167 ff. See also II, p. 484 ff. and X, p. 384.
[2] *ibid.*, III, p. 171.

general attitude, for if fasting becomes an end in itself, it may easily lead to pride. Perhaps we need to apply the word in a wider sense to-day; its spirit is exemplified in going without something in order to benefit someone else, in sacrificing time used for one's own pleasure in order to help those in need. Such actions may express the idea behind fasting, without implying that abstention from food may not be useful.

How should Christians observe Sunday? It is a question which caused arguments in the seventeenth century, as it does in our own era. Taylor looks at the subject positively when he says that the Jewish day of rest is changed into one of activity for Christians. We abstain from work in order to attend to our religion. Though the constraint to keep the fourth commandment does not apply in quite the same sense to us as to the Jews, we have more reason than they to honour God. We should abstain from all works unless they are of great necessity or of great charity. Yet it is not to be a day of idleness: 'It is better to plough upon holy days than to do nothing or to do viciously.' It is to be primarily a day of joyous festivity on which we attend Holy Communion and public worship. Between the services we may use the time to visit the sick, help the poor and reconcile differences. Recreations should not produce wantonness, drunkenness, quarrelling or ridiculous or superstitious behaviour. Beyond that there is to be Christian liberty. 'He keeps the Lord's day best, that keeps it with the most religion and the most charity.'[1]

Taylor has much to say about the subject of prayer in various places in his writings and, though only the briefest summary is possible, it is obvious that it occupied an important place in his thinking. The number of his own prayers scattered throughout his writings is further evidence of the value that he attached to it. Prayer is not only a duty we owe to God but it is an act of grace that we are permitted to approach Him in this way. God has promised to hear us

[1] *ibid.*, III, p. 171 ff;. II, p. 430 ff.; III, p. 11.

and in addition has appointed His Son to make intercession for us. He has given men through prayer the ability to alter His decrees: it has saved cities, raised the dead and altered the course of nature. 'It cures diseases without physic, and makes physic do the work of nature, and nature do the work of grace, and grace do the work of God, and it does miracles of accident and event.'[1]

We must pass over a detailed account of the sixteen rules which Taylor gives about prayer, including what to pray for, the relation of prayer to life, the length of prayer in public and private, times of prayer and even posture in prayer, and select two aspects on which he gives particularly sound advice. The first concerns wandering thoughts. We are to ask for the spirit of prayer, but we may help ourselves in private devotions by using collects or short forms of prayer, repeating those prayers in which we failed to concentrate. In public prayer this last device is not possible, but we may say Amen with heartiness, even if we have not followed closely every clause of the prayer. In this connection Taylor warns his readers against too many worldly cares, for these may cause our thoughts to stray. He stresses too the value of praying silently: 'For in mental prayer if our thoughts wander, we only stand still; when our mind returns, we go on again: there is none of the prayer lost, as it is if our mouths speak and our hearts wander.'[2]

The other hindrance to prayer is tediousness of spirit. Here again remedies are suggested. We are not to let our prayers become tedious through their being too long; we can retain the matter while reducing the number of words. Variety is a help; a hymn may be recited when a collect seems flat. As with wandering thoughts, the breaking up of prayers into fragments is of benefit, and this would seem to imply the breaking up of times of prayer too; Taylor says that by praying often we may make everything relish of religion.[3]

[1] *Works*, III, p. 176.   [2] *ibid.*, p. 183. See also II, pp. 477-83.
[3] *ibid.*, p. 184 f. Similar advice is to be found in the preface to Taylor's *Collection of Offices*.

Just as the aid of the Holy Spirit is necessary in the reading of the Bible, so we need it in our prayers. Praying in the Spirit means praying in His strength according to His purposes. It is the Spirit Who gives an appetite to our prayers; those who pray merely out of custom or unwillingly have not the Spirit of Christ. The Spirit helps us in our weaknesses giving us confidence and importunity.[1] Taylor's general attitude may best be summed up in his own words: 'Prayer is one of the noblest exercises of christian religion, or rather it is that duty in which all graces are concentrated. Prayer is charity, it is faith, it is a conformity to God's will, a desiring according to the desires of heaven, an imitation of Christ's intercession, and prayer must suppose all holiness, or else it is nothing: and therefore all that in which men need God's spirit, all that is in order to prayer. Baptism is but a prayer and the holy sacrament of the Lord's supper is but a prayer; a prayer of sacrifice representative, and a prayer of oblation, and a prayer of intercession, and a prayer of thanksgiving. And obedience is a prayer, and begs and procures blessings: and if the Holy Ghost hath sanctified the whole man, then He hath sanctified the prayer of the man, and not till then.'[2]

Taylor interprets almsgiving in its widest sense. Mercy, Beneficence or Welldoing, Liberality and Charity are, he says, the four twin-daughters of their mother Alms. He gives a comprehensive list of all that may be included under the general title of works of mercy in which, along with the more usual ones, figure such acts as mending bridges and highways and paying maidens' dowries. Spiritual acts are enumerated and include such actions as counselling the doubtful and warning sinners. The kind of almsgiving which combines spiritual and temporal ends includes erecting schools of learning and putting children to honest trades.

[1] From a sermon on 'The spirit of prayers and supplication'. (*Works*, IV, p. 342 ff.)
[2] *Works*, IV, p. 346 f.

As usual, Taylor is ready with a list of rules to guide the Christian in performing this duty. First, of course, we are to give what is our own. Money gained for work done unlawfully on Sunday or hire for being a professed jester may be given when the offender has repented. Alms are to be given secretly to those in need, but not in such a way as to encourage misuse. They are to be given cheerfully. Taylor is anxious that the wealthy should give in charity what is superfluous to their estates, but he recognizes that the owner has responsibilities to the future as well as to the present. He believes that sometimes the standard of living is unnecessarily luxurious but, with his host in mind perhaps, adds: 'But this is only intended to be an advice in the manner of doing alms: for I am not ignorant that great variety of clothes always have been permitted to princes and nobility, and others in their proportion; and they usually give these clothes as rewards to servants, and other persons needful enough, and then they may serve their own fancy and their duty too: but it is but reason and religion that they be given to such only where duty, or prudent liberality, or alms determine them: but in no sense let them do it so as to minister to vanity, to luxury, to prodigality.'[1]

In giving to 'beggars and persons of low rank' it is better to give a little to each. In the case of colleges, hospitals and houses of devotion and supplying the needs of 'decayed persons fallen from great plenty to great necessity' it is wiser to give large sums. It is not essential to be concerned with every kind of charity; if we prefer to feed the poor, we are not obliged to redeem captives, though we must respond to need as we come across it. If we have no money we ought to possess great mercy and pity. Every Christian should do what he can, 'be it little or great, corporal or spiritual, the charity of alms or the charity of prayers, a cup of wine or a cup of water, if it be but love to the brethren, or a desire to help all or any of Christ's poor, it shall be accepted

[1] *Works*, III, p. 192.

according to what a man hath, not according to what he hath not.'[1]

It would be fair to say that charity in all its aspects occupied an important place in Taylor's thought. Much of his teaching came from his own experience of the miseries of the times in which he lived. In this connection we may quote some words of Mr Douglas Bush: 'And since Taylor has been accused of ignoring all but the well-fed, it may be added that he often contrasts virtuous poverty with sinful wealth and is aware of the oppression and "the needs of the poor man, his rent day and the cryes of his children".'[2] If some of Taylor's notions are dated, there are others which are equally applicable to-day. The age which condemns the snobbery of birth has substituted a snobbery of wealth and position.

We may pass over the subject of repentance which Taylor amplified in *Unum Necessarium* some years later, and which has been dealt with fully earlier in this book, and turn now to his guidance about receiving the Sacrament. Though there has been some discussion about the variety of his views, at no time would it be true to say that he underestimated its importance.[3] Taylor's rules are of interest.[4] There must be repentance of known sin and examination of the soul to search out secret ulcers. This should lead the individual to those whom the Great Physician has appointed to minister to our diseases. Evil affections are to be expelled; time is to be set aside for good actions, for repentance and prayer for pardon; injuries are to be forgiven, and those whom we have offended are to be reconciled. Fasting, prayers and abstinence from secular pleasures are other ways of preparation. Except in the case of sickness, there is to be fasting before Communion. Taylor gives advice on how to receive the elements and stresses the importance of faith, of partaking worthily and of not enquiring too closely into the mystery: 'It is

---

[1] *ibid.*, p. 194. See also IV, p. 171 ff.; II, p. 459 ff.; III, p. 303.
[2] *English Literature in the Earlier Seventeen Century*, p. 317.
[3] Much of what he says in *Holy Living* is repeated in *The Worthy Communicant*.
[4] See also *Works*, VIII, p. 154 ff.

sufficient to thee that Christ shall be present to thy soul as an instrument of grace, as a pledge of the resurrection, as the earnest of glory and immortality, and as a means of many intermediate blessings, even all such as are necessary for thee and are in order to thy salvation.'[1]

After reminding the communicant that Christ dwells within him, Taylor goes on to suggest that the rest of the day should be spent in 'entertaining your blessed Lord with all the caresses and sweetness of love . . . and as the affairs of your person or employment call you off, so retire again with often ejaculations and acts of entertainment to your beloved guest'.[2] Taylor concludes by stressing the value of Communion both to the Church and the individual. The Church is nourished in faith, hope and love and the members are joined through it to one another and to Christ. He by His death, resurrection and intercession in heaven for us has purchased for us 'long life and health, and recovery from sickness, and competent support and maintenance, and peace and deliverance from our enemies, and content, and patience and joy, and sanctified riches, or a cheerful poverty, and liberty, and whatsoever else is a blessing'. In the Sacrament we may receive any of these. All should come: the sinner having forsaken his sin, the convert that he may grow in grace, the mature because he has the right disposition, those with leisure because they have no reason for not coming, and those without leisure that their business may be sanctified.

Though it is outside the scope of Taylor's list of internal acts, it is not inappropriate to include in this section what he has to say on the subject of public worship, for one of the duties which he connects with observance of the Lord's day is attendance at the services. We shall look first at the importance he attaches to the liturgy and then at the place of preaching. There is no doubt that Taylor was a strong upholder of liturgical forms of worship. It will be remembered that he produced his own *Collection of Offices* when the

---

[1] *Works*, III, p. 218.   [2] *ibid.*, p. 219.

Puritans substituted *The Directory* for the *Book of Common Prayer*; Taylor desired the retention of liturgical forms. The prayers in this *Collection*, he says 'are (especially in the chiefest offices) collected out of the devotions of the Greek Church with some mixture of Mozarabic and Ethiopic and other liturgies, and perfected out of the fountains of Scripture, and therefore for the material part have warrant and great authority: and therefore if they be used with submission to authority, it is hoped they may do good'.[1] The book itself is comprehensive in scope containing, in addition to the order of morning and evening prayer, collects for use on a wide variety of occasions.

Taylor had positive reasons for preferring liturgies to extempore prayer and though his *Apology for Authorized and Set Forms of Liturgy* contains thirty-one indictments of *The Directory*, on the positive side he stresses, for example, the suitability of the different forms of absolution at Matins and Evensong, the visitation of the sick and in the Communion Order.[2]

The chief bone of contention was the subject of extempore prayer. At some length Taylor sets out his convictions that all the evidence from Scripture and tradition is in favour of set forms. Those in the *Prayer Book*, he says, are hallowed by usage and the authority of the Church, guided by the Spirit of God. Christ Himself gave a form of prayer to His disciples. If the Puritans argued that set forms restrained the Spirit, Taylor's answer was that extempore prayer did not necessarily make for liberty. There could be freedom and restraint in both types.[3] Would those who pray extempore be willing to preach and to sing hymns by the same method? Members of a congregation may follow the set prayers and know what they are about and to what they give assent with their Amen; extempore prayer might lead to speech without thought and estimating the quality of the prayer according to its length. The Puritans were of the opinion that extempore prayer was more true to the pattern of the New Testament and regarded

[1] *ibid.*, VIII, p. 573.   [2] *ibid.*, V, p. 251.   [3] *ibid.*, p. 307.

the Lord's Prayer as model rather than a set form. Some of them believed that liturgies made it possible for errors to be perpetuated, and that they might also deprive the ministers and people of the gift of prayer, since they could not meet the needs of differing needs and occasions. They accused the supporters of set forms of believing that God could be worshipped in one way only, and feared the formalism which repetition might produce.[1]

Within the context of worship the sermon, according to Taylor, occupies an important place for it is one half of the minister's office and employment. Sermons are to be particular rather than general and are not to be dictated by the wishes of the congregation: 'Let not the humours and inclinations of the people be the measures of your doctrines, but let your doctrines be the measure of their persuasions.'[2] The business of the sermon is to preach a holy life, obedience, peace and love for our neighbours. Backbiting and intemperance are to be dealt with severely. The most frequent themes are to be: death, judgement, heaven and hell, the life and death of Jesus Christ, God's mercy to repenting sinners and His severity against the impenitent. Baxter's advice is very similar to Taylor's, revealing how little sympathy they both have with the idea that the pulpit is merely a place for oratory.[3]

The difference between the Puritans and Taylor is to be found in the latter's allusions, metaphors and similes which are lacking generally in Puritan preaching. As Professor Horton Davies has said: 'Since the Puritans confined themselves to simple, serious, evangelical preaching, we look in vain for certain characteristics in their sermons. The wit of South, the brilliant and quaint imaginations of Donne, the sustained metaphors of Jeremy Taylor or the racy language of Latimer, are not to be found there. These qualities are less obtrusive.'[4]

---

[1] See Prof. Horton Davies, *The Worship of the English Puritans*, p. 98.
[2] *Works*, I, p. 107.   [3] R. Baxter, *Works*, iii, p. 25.
[4] *The Worship of the English Puritans*, p. 203.

Nevertheless, to see Taylor's preaching in antithesis to that of the Puritans would be misleading, as if beauty of imagery or fine prose obscured his message. A glance at the titles of his sermons is sufficient to show that he chose great themes. He brought to the pulpit not only a zealous heart but an enlightened mind, and sought to enrich and clarify the truths which he declared. He may have lacked the vehemence of some Puritan preachers, but there is no disputing his underlying seriousness of spirit or that he saw in the sermon a means of guiding and building up the faith of Christians. 'Hooker', says Professor Horton Davies, 'looks askance upon sermons as the corrupt production of men, whilst the reading of Scripture preserves the Word of God unadulterated.' If there is an isolated passage from Taylor which might appear to support this thesis, there is plenty of contrary evidence, both in precept and practice, to show that he went beyond Hooker in viewing the sermon as an extension of the Word of God.[1]

There has been a tendency in modern times to regard the Church of England as the home of worship and the Free Church as a preaching centre. Perhaps the link between the Anglican Church and the State has helped to contribute to an order and ceremonial that is everywhere the same — though this statement may need some modification to-day. The Free Church has often represented the 'gathered community' type of church which produces a greater freedom in forms of prayer and a stronger emphasis on exhortation. Each has something to contribute to the other. The importance which Taylor attaches to both liturgies and the sermon suggests that he attempted, not unsuccessfully, to achieve a synthesis between the worship of God and His word to man.

2. THE DEVELOPMENT OF CHRISTIAN CHARACTER

We turn in this section to a consideration of Christian character and its connection with the cardinal virtues of

[1] See *Works*, III, p. 164 ff.

I

prudence, temperance and fortitude. Two well-known statements: 'Talents are developed in solitude but character in the stream of life' and 'Man is only man in relation to God and his fellows' remind us that it is not possible ultimately to view the character of the Christian in isolation. Yet, recognizing the limitations, for the purposes of this study we may do so if we ask what kind of a person the Christian should be in himself. How does he spend his time? What motives determine his actions? Is he the master or the slave of his passions? How does he face hardship and suffering? No doubt it is through both his religious life and his fellowship with others that he finds the answers to these questions, and the extent to which he does so will determine his usefulness to God and man. Nevertheless, it will be seen that these questions do provide a basis for examining the development of Christian character as a subject in its own right, remembering that the cardinal virtues will be strengthened in the individual as he develops and exercises the theological virtues of faith, hope and love.

We know that the cardinal virtues were classical rather than Christian in origin. With other classical ideas they were baptized into Christianity and given thereby a richer and fuller meaning. To-day they are interpreted in a variety of ways. Some regard them as virtues which in themselves are worthy of development; Christians think of them in relation to God. One other point ought to be mentioned by way of introduction. Faith, hope and love were linked with the cognitive, affective and conative aspects of experience respectively; we may find a similar link between prudence and the mind, temperance and feelings, and fortitude and the will. But, as with the theological virtues, the caution must be sounded that such links are suitable only for purposes of analysis.

We shall begin with prudence. Many people regard this virtue as nothing more than sound judgement. If a man is neither rash nor impetuous, if he exercises caution with respect to the present and forethought about the future, he

is said to be prudent. There are others who describe as
prudent the person who has a moral end in his choices and
acts. Though the Christian would not deny that these
definitions may be included in the virtue, he goes further in
thinking of it as 'the habit of referring all questions, whether
of ideals or of courses of action, to the criterion of God's will
for us.'[1]

Taylor does not say explicitly in *Holy Living* that he is
going to describe prudence, yet he can hardly have intended
to omit it. A close examination of the first chapter suggests
that when he writes of the care of our time, purity of intention
and the practice of the presence of God, he is thinking of
Christian prudence. Such a treatment of the virtue would
fit suitably the definition quoted above of referring everything to the criterion of God's will for us. Indeed this is
implied in the opening words of the first chapter: 'It is
necessary that every man should consider, that since God
hath given him an excellent nature, wisdom and choice, an
understanding soul and an immortal spirit, having made
him lord over the beasts, and but a little lower than the
angels; He hath also appointed for him a work and a service
great enough to employ those abilities, and hath also
designed him to a state of life after this, to which he can only
arrive by that service and obedience: and therefore as every
man is wholly God's own portion by the title of creation, so
all our labours and care, all our powers and faculties, must
be wholly employed in the service of God, even all the days
of our life; that this life being ended, we may live with Him
for ever.'[2] The way to arrive at the end of glory, he says, is
'by all the ways of grace, prudence, and religion'.

The first means of achieving this end is by the care of our
time. Taylor stresses that the time of preparation for eternity
is short, but he does not regard this as a hindrance since
secular responsibilities may be viewed as sacred duties: 'No
man can complain that his calling takes him off from

---

[1] K. E. Kirk, *Some Principles of Moral Theology*, p. 34 f.
[2] *Works*, III, p. 7.

religion: his calling itself and his very worldly employment
in honest trades and offices is a serving of God.' Because he
believes idleness to be the parent of many evils, Taylor gives
rules for the employment of our time.[1]

The day is to begin and end with God and the intervening
time is to be filled suitably. It is particularly important that
leisure should be used properly; companions who might
tempt us to misuse it are to be avoided. The work that we
do ought to be such as is suitable to our persons and callings,
and consistent with our Christian profession. It is possible
to be too fastidious about appearances; there are some who
'comb out all their opportunities of their morning devotion'.
Moderation is to be used in recreation and long waiting upon
important persons is to be avoided. Taylor is also an uncompromising opponent of gossip. It is necessary to set aside
time every day for prayer when outside interests should not
be allowed to intrude. At night time it is useful to recall all
the events of the day. The habit of turning our thoughts to
prayer during the day may be encouraged by letting the
striking of the clock act as a reminder. Those who are busiest
should set aside a time each year for what to-day would be
called 'a retreat'. Taylor, nevertheless, cautions his readers
about being over-scrupulous about minutes; it is general
principles with which he is concerned. To observe such rules,
he says, would save us from the sins which spring from
idleness: lying, flattery, stealing, dissimulation and the sins
of the flesh. They would help us to do positive good so that
we are prepared at 'the sudden coming of the Lord'.

We are reminded even more forcibly of our definition of
prudence in Taylor's teaching about purity of intention
which, he says, demands that we should design and intend
God's glory in every action. Unless we have this attitude
even our best deeds are worthless because the motive is
wrong. In the rules which follow, Taylor urges us to think
about the reasons for our actions. If there is some temptation

[1] *Works*, III, p. 10-15. See Appendix for the use John Wesley made of these
rules.

which would mar the purpose of our duty, we are to purify the purpose and not omit the duty. He reminds us that it is not necessary to set all temporal actions in opposition to those which are spiritual.[1] Amongst the signs of purity of intention are: valuing a religious design before a temporal; disregarding the censures of men; doing as well in private as in public; praying to God and leaving the results to Him; rejoicing even in our failures, if they enhance the glory of God.[2]

The third means of exercising the virtue of prudence, in the sense in which we have defined it, is by the practice of the presence of God.[3] Though God may be found everywhere, He is especially present in some places. If men would only remember the omnipresence of God, sin would soon cease, for He is present by His glory in heaven, in the meetings of His servants, in the hearts of His people by His Holy Spirit and in the consciences of all. As usual, Taylor provides rules to help his readers to put into practice the teaching which he has just given.[4] Everything is to remind us of God: 'In the face of the sun you may see God's beauty; in the fire you may find His heat warming; in the water, His gentleness to refresh you . . .' Since God is within us we should not deface His workmanship. He is in every creature; we are to be cruel to none. To practise such an attitude would, Taylor believes, help prayer, give confidence, joy and rejoicing in God, develop humility, restrain wandering thoughts and establish the heart in good purposes: 'What a child would do in the eye of his father, and a pupil before his tutor, and a wife in the presence of her husband, and a servant in the sight of his master, let us do the same . . . we are always in the sight and presence of the all-seeing and almighty God, who also is to us a father and a guardian, a husband and a lord.'[5] Taylor adds some prayers which he states would not take much more than half-an-hour to say: 'By affording to God one hour in twenty-four, thou mayest

[1] ibid., III, p. 16-19.   [2] ibid., p. 19-21.   [3] ibid., p. 22 ff.
[4] ibid., p. 25-7.   [5] ibid., p. 29.

have the comforts and rewards of devotion: but he that thinks this is too much, either is very busy in the world, or very careless of heaven.'[1]

We have seen enough to sustain the suggestion that Taylor's introduction to *Holy Living* comes within the scope of prudence. This is supported by his teaching elsewhere: 'It is the duty of christian prudence to choose the end of a Christian, that which is perfective of a man, satisfactory to reason, the rest of a Christian, and the beatification of his spirit; and that is, to choose and desire and propound to himself heaven and the fruition of God as the end of all his acts and arts, his designs and purposes.'[2] The theme is developed to include the more general sense of prudence. In his emphasis upon avoiding indiscreet zeal and the value of a spiritual guide, he quotes Socrates with approval: 'Virtue is but a shadow and a servile employment, unless it be adorned and instructed with prudence.'[3]

It will be seen that prudence is a virtue not only in its own right but in its influence upon the way in which other virtues are exercised. It prevents temperance, fortitude and justice from becoming ends in themselves rather than a means to an end. It may, of course, be argued that prudence itself might become nothing more than excessive caution; this is only possible with the derivatives of prudence and not with the virtue as it is defined at the beginning of this section.

In turning to temperance, we remember that, as with prudence, the Christian will define it with regard to its end. Restraint may be exercised for a variety of reasons: the athlete wishes to excel at some sport or game, the patient wants to make a speedy recovery from his illness, the old man desires to prolong his life. Such restraint may be based upon reason, but, if we are to separate the aspects of experience, we see from the examples given what a force desire may be. The end commends itself to the mind of man but,

[1] *Works*, III, p. 42.
[2] *ibid.*, IV, p. 575 f. (From a sermon on Christian Prudence, IV, 573 ff.). See also II, p. 291.
[3] *ibid.*, IV, p. 608.

unless there is an emotional driving force which moves the will, habits of intemperance prevail. Temperance may be exercised quite apart from religion in the instances given. It may be viewed from a moral as distinct from a religious angle by the person who abhors excess in any shape or form. Behaviour which involves excess he regards as unbecoming; temperance in such a man springs from a code of conduct which he has absorbed from his environment or chosen for himself.

The Christian definition of temperance implies a self-control which is exercised because we believe that we have been bought with a price and that we are to glorify God in our bodies: they are to be presented as living sacrifices to Him Who redeemed us body and soul. It is a self-control imposed so that we may be of the utmost service to God and to our fellows. Taylor calls it sobriety and he defines it as 'a using severity, denial and frustration of our appetite, when it grows unreasonable' with respect to meat and drink, pleasures and thoughts. He plans to help the Christian to achieve temperance in food and drink, chastity, humility and modesty.[1] Sobriety is opposed to sensuality in three ways, he says: it is a resolve against it, a fight against it, and a delight in spiritual things. His practical advice includes limiting desire to necessity, suppressing the first approach of sensual desires by turning from them to some useful employment, thinking of the sorrow that results from over-indulgence and concentrating in thought upon the joys of heaven. It is also a help to recall the example of Christ and His apostles, of Moses and wise men.

In referring to the particular acts of Christian sobriety, Taylor begins with temperance in meat and drink. 'Sobriety is the bridle of the passions of desire, and temperance is the bit and curb of that bridle, a restraint put into a man's mouth, a moderate use of meat and drink, so as may best consist with our health, and may not hinder but help the works of the soul by its necessary supporting us, and ministering cheerfulness and refreshment.'[2] For the healthy there

<hr>

[1] *ibid.*, III, p. 44.   [2] *ibid.*, p. 47.

will be enjoyment in eating and drinking but pleasure will not be the end. Though at festivals or in private celebrations the more pleasant may be chosen as being more nourishable or digestible, the choice must not be abused.

Taylor gives some simple rules which the modern reader may find rather trite. They do, however, throw an interesting light on the age in which Taylor lived and some of the people whom he must have met. He says that there should be no eating between meals unless there is a special reason. Food should not be eaten hastily, nor should there be fussiness about its choice: 'It is lawful in all senses to comply with a weak and a nice stomach, but not with a nice and curious palate.'[1] The signs of a temperate man are these: he is modest, for greediness is unmannerly and rude; he is grave of deportment; he has a sound but moderate sleep, he rises early; he has a suppressed and seldom anger; a command of his thoughts and passions, and he speaks little about food and drink.[2] Taylor draws his picture and without a great deal of imagination we can see in it a portrait of himself.

It is unnecessary for us to follow the detailed account of drunkenness and its evil consequences which Taylor gives. His rules for the temperate life include a strict judgement about the extra glass which makes a man incapable of discerning his condition. Something of the appetite is to be left unfilled and no man is to be urged to eat or drink beyond his own limit or desire. To abstain from gluttony and drunkenness, we are to remind ourselves, is part of the faith of a disciple of Jesus Christ. Grace before meals and pious conversation during them will help. We are to be careful not to be brought under the power of meat, drink or smoke.[3]

Taylor begins his section on chastity with a warning. Some men, he says, study cases of conscience about carnal sins, not to avoid evil but to learn how to offend God and pollute their own spirits: 'If any man will snatch the pure taper from my hand and hold it to the devil, he will only burn

[1] *Works*, III, p. 49.   [2] *ibid.*, p. 50.   [3] *ibid.*, p. 55, cp. II, p. 180 ff.

his own fingers.'[1] In defining chastity Taylor takes an ortho-
dox line and though he sees virtues in celibacy, he does not
feel that it is a superior state to matrimony; some married
people are better than some celibates. He deals in detail
with the evil consequences of impurity and includes two
quotations from the New Testament in support of chastity:
our bodies are the temples of the Holy Spirit, and marriage
is used as a picture of the union of Christ with His Church.
It is perhaps worth noting, in view of other attitudes which
have been held, that Taylor regards adultery as worse in a
man than in a woman 'who is of a more pliant and easy
spirit'. In respect of its effects, it is worse in a woman. In
relation to God the sin is equally damnable in either case.
Taylor has a list of acts of chastity and provides rules for
virgins, widows and married couples. His remedies against
uncleanness are practical: they include fleeing from temptation rather than arguing with it; mortification — a spare
diet, for example, may be useful sometimes; prayer; meditation on the Divine presence, death and the Cross.[2]

Taylor obviously attaches great importance to humility.
There are references to it in many places in his writings. He
regards it as one of the fruits of temperance and calls it 'the
great ornament and jewel of christian religion'. Its opposite
is pride and Taylor devotes some space to arguments against
this contrary vice. He reminds his readers that man's
strength is inferior to that of many animals and his beauty
less than that of numerous flowers. The best learning teaches
humility; to be proud of knowledge is a sign of the greatest
ignorance. Pride in riches is foolish; a gold mine is superior
in this respect to the possessor of wealth. If a man excels
spiritually, he should remember that all souls are equal. If
we are worse than our neighbours we are to blame ourselves;
if we are better, we must remember that God is the author
of our goodness.

Taylor gives nineteen acts of humility.[3] He includes in his
injunctions the advice not to consider ourselves better than

[1] ibid., III, p. 55. [2] ibid., p. 60 ff. See also II, p. 442 ff. [3] ibid., III, p. 70 ff.

others because of outward circumstances. We are to be content for others to think the evil which we admit about ourselves. We are to welcome being thought little of and are not to be ashamed of our birth, trade or poverty. We should neither attempt to gain praise by self-depreciation nor practice vanity. We are to rejoice when others are praised in our presence and not attempt to disparage them, and we should never compare ourselves with others unless it is to their advantage. Various rules and exercises follow.[1]

We may wonder whether Taylor is right in urging us to call our worst sins to mind every day, though he does say that this is useful when we are tempted to pride. Frequent confession, praying for grace, meditation on pride and humility are other exercises mentioned. Taylor makes a shrewd point when he says that as we often disparage others whom we hear commended, in similar circumstances we ought to be as strict with ourselves. Realizing the great danger of spiritual pride, he urges the value of thinking of the humility of Christ. The flatterer should not be tolerated and we should not pretend to be studying or praying when a visitor arrives! The value of confession in developing humility is also mentioned. It is worth while quoting Taylor's 'signs of humility' in full:

'The humble man trusts not to his own discretion, but in matters of concernment relies rather upon the judgement of his friends, counsellors, or spiritual guides; he does not pertinaciously pursue the choice of his own will, but in all things lets God choose for him, and his superiors in those things which concern them; he does not murmur against commands; he is not inquisitive into the reasonableness of indifferent and innocent commands, but believes their command to be reason enough in such cases to exact his obedience; he lives according to a rule, and with compliance to public customs, without any affectation or singularity; he is meek and indifferent in all accidents and chances; he patiently bears injuries; he is always unsatisfied in his own

---

[1] *Works*, III, p. 74.

conduct, resolutions, and counsels; he is a great lover of good men, and a praiser of wise men, and a censurer of no man; he is modest in his speech and reserved in his laughter; he fears when he hears himself commended, lest God make another judgement concerning his actions than men do; he gives no pert or saucy answers when he is reproved, whether justly or unjustly; he loves to sit down in private, and, if he may, he refuses the temptation of offices and new honours; he is ingenuous, free, and open, in his actions and discourses; he mends his fault, and gives thanks, when he is admonished; he is ready to do good offices to the murderers of his fame, to his slanderers, backbiters, and detractors, as Christ washed the feet of Judas; and is contented to be suspected of indiscretion, so before God he may be really innocent, and not offensive to his neighbour, nor wanting to his just and prudent interest.'[1]

Here is a picture of the kind of Christian that Taylor would have liked to see multiplied. If we feel that there is not enough self-reliance in the make-up of this character, we must remember that Taylor himself does not give the impression at this period of his life of possessing this quality in abundance. He was a poor chaplain in a great house, and no doubt suffered from some of the disadvantages of that position. Yet this type of character has frequently commended itself to men more readily than the more forceful characters that tend to be opinionated. Pride, as G. K. Chesterton has pointed out, is a sin men will not tolerate easily in others.

Thomas Fuller in his quaint essays and characters does not go quite as far as Taylor. 'Self-praising comes most naturally from a man when it comes most violently from him in his own defence — for though modesty binds a man's tongue to the peace in this point, yet being assaulted in his credit, he may stand upon his guard, and then he doth not so much praise as purge himself. One braved a gentleman to his face, that in skill and valour he came far behind him.

[1] *ibid.*, p. 78. See also II, p. 628 ff.

"It is true," said the other, "for when I fought with you, you ran away before me." In such a case, it was well returned, and without any just aspersion of pride'.[1] Baxter on the other hand is nearer to Taylor: 'Art thou one that much valuest the applause of the people? and feelest thy heart tickle with delight when thou hearest of thy great esteem with men; and much dejected when thou hearest that men slight thee? . . . Art thou ready to quarrel with every man that lets fall a word in derogation from thy honour?' Baxter asks many questions of this sort and says if the answer is in the affirmative the reader is a proud person.[2]

Taylor turns next to modesty which he describes as 'the appendage of sobriety, and is to charity, to temperance, and to humility, as the fringes are to a garment. . . (It) is directly opposed to curiosity, to boldness, to undecency'. He begins by giving acts of modesty as opposed to acts of boldness: 'Enquire not into the secrets of God, but be content to learn thy duty according to the quality of thy person or employment . . . .' There is to be a lack of curiosity about things which are too difficult for us to understand and we are not to be inquisitive about the affairs of others which are no concern of ours. Listening at doors and windows, opening the letters of other people without a very good reason are some of the more commonplace instructions that Taylor gives.[3] Immodesty may be revealed by a casual attitude to natural calamities which Taylor viewed as judgements of God. To be merry on the shore when there is a tempest to be observed over the sea or to dance when it is thundering are examples which he gives of disregarding when God speaks.

Light is thrown possibly on Taylor's position as a household chaplain in the next rule: 'Be reverent, modest, and reserved, in the presence of thy betters, giving to all according to their quality their titles of honour, keeping distance,

[1] Thomas Fuller, *The Holy State and The Profane State*, p. 147 f.
[2] Richard Baxter, *The Saints' Rest*, II, p. 197 f.
[3] *Works*, III, p. 79 f.

speaking little, answering pertinently, not interposing without leave or reason, not answering to a question propounded to another; and ever present to thy superiors the fairest side of thy discourse, of thy temper, of thy ceremony, as being ashamed to serve excellent persons with unhandsome intercourse.'[1] We should never lie to a king or a great person, nor should we try to justify a fault. We are not to boast of sin, be confident in uncertain matters or pretend to greater knowledge than we possess.

In his acts of modesty, Taylor urges the appropriate demeanour on all occasions. We are to 'abstain from wanton and dissolute laughter, petulant and uncomely jests, loud talking, jeering, and all such actions, which in civil account, are called undecencies and incivilities'.[2] Clothing and ornament are to be grave. Servants are to be made to feel that their normal diligence gives pleasure to their masters: 'For the man or woman that is dressed with anger and impatience, wears pride under their robes, and immodesty above.' Affected walking, ridiculous gestures and the use of cosmetics are all condemned. Things outside natural and moral interest, such as spectacles, theatres, loud noises and outcries are to be avoided. This modesty of demeanour is to be extended to the treatment of our bodies. Taylor writes with interest, but the modern reader is left with an impression of a treatise on good manners.

In examining Taylor's teaching about fortitude, we are reminded that, as in the case of prudence and temperance, this cardinal virtue may be defined in different ways. Some will think of it as the stoical endurance of trouble, as perseverance against great difficulties or even as an act of defiance against overwhelming odds. The Christian would not deny the element of both active and passive endurance which the word fortitude conjures up, but as with the other virtues, he would demand that we look at it with regard to its end. It is the conquest by the spirit of all which prevents us persevering in the will of God for our lives. It looks beyond the

[1] *ibid.*, p. 81.　　　　[2] *ibid.*, p. 82.

seen and temporal to the unseen and eternal. It is not surprising that if for analytical purposes prudence is linked with intellect and temperance with desire, fortitude should be connected with the will. While we must admit that Taylor links fortitude with temperance and calls it contentedness, we are doing no violence to his thought in separating it, for it is implicit in his writings that it is nothing less than Christian fortitude that he is describing.

Taylor makes it clear at the start that contentedness implies co-operation with God Who orders the universe. God is the master of the scene; we are not to choose the part which we are to act. Having given up our will to Him, we are to let God choose for us and to stand in that station of the battle where our great general has placed us. 'We are in the world like men playing at tables; the chance is not in our power, but to play it is; and when it is fallen we must manage it as we can . . . Therefore if thou hast lost thy land, do not also lose thy constancy: and if thou must die a little sooner, yet do not die impatiently . . . No man can make another man to be his slave unless he hath first enslaved himself to life and death, to pleasure or pain, to hope or fear; command these passions, and you are freer than the Parthian kings.' These analogies give some idea of the way in which Taylor thinks of fortitude.[1]

To procure contentedness, troubles may be turned to spiritual advantage. 'If thou art out of favour with thy prince, secure the favour of the King of kings, and then there is no harm come to thee.'[2] We may think of those with whom we would not change places rather than those who are better off than we are, while to count our past and present blessings is a help. The following passage looks as it if were autobiographical: 'I am fallen into the hands of publicans and sequestrators, and they have taken all from me: what now? let me look about me. They have left me the sun and the moon, fire and water, a loving wife, and many friends to pity me, and some to relieve me, and I can still discourse;

[1] *Works*, III, p. 85 ff.   [2] *ibid.*, p. 88.

and unless I list they have not taken away my merry countenance, and my cheerful spirit, and a good conscience: they have still left me the providence of God, and all the promises of the gospel, and my religion and my hopes of heaven, and my charity to them too; and still I can sleep and digest, I eat and drink, I read and meditate, I can walk in my neighbour's pleasant fields, and see the variety of natural beauties, and delight in all that in which God delights, that is, in virtue and wisdom, in the whole creation, and in God himself.'[1]

Enjoyment of the present without anxiety about the future is the best means to secure contentedness. We are to measure our desire by our fortunes, and not our fortunes by our desires: 'Is that beast better that hath two or three mountains to graze on, than a little bee that feeds on dew or manna, and lives on what falls every morning from the storehouses of heaven, clouds and providence?'[2] Some evils, Taylor holds, are better than their contraries, and to a good man the very worst is tolerable. The chapter concludes with counsels to aid Christians in particular troubles including poverty, the charge of many children, violent necessities, the death of children, nearest relatives or friends, untimely death, being childless, evil or unfortunate children.[3] If the word fortitude is not used, the idea is present.

It has been possible to deal only in the barest outline with this aspect of fortitude — a willingness to say with St Paul: 'I have learned, in whatsoever state I am, therewith to be content.' There are other conditions besides the loss of material prosperity when fortitude is required. Suffering is one example. In a sermon on 'The faith and patience of the saints; or the righteous cause oppressed', Taylor argues that the state of the gospel is a state of suffering and not of temporal prosperity, even as Christ suffered from His birth to His death.[4] The Christian, God has promised, will be

[1] ibid., p. 91.   [2] ibid., p. 94.
[3] ibid., p. 101 ff. On poverty, see also II, p. 67, 391 ff. and 343, IV, p. 549 ff.
[4] ibid., IV, p. 431 ff.

sustained in his suffering, not exempted from it. If the saints did not suffer, God would lose the glory of bringing good out of evil, of being with them in tribulation, of sustaining them and enabling them to triumph over the malice of their enemies. These are reasons which many would regard as suspect to-day. In his rules Taylor urges his readers to pray for their persecutors and to accept their sufferings in a Christian spirit.

The more common use of the word suffering is in its association with illness, and fortitude is needed here perhaps even more than in persecution. In the case of oppression others may share the suffering, and there may be a sense of the glory of martyrdom which lifts the spirit to a higher level. The patient is likely to feel alone in his battle and can seldom regard his pain as suffering in a righteous cause. Taylor devoted a whole book to Christian behaviour in illness and *The Rule and Exercises of Holy Dying* became a classic. In the seventeenth century, because of the lack of medical skill and the short expectation of life, death occupied a prominent place in men's thought; sickness was regarded as the ante-chamber of death. Taylor, as is evident from his work devoted to the subject, does not neglect this aspect of experience but, in general, he shows a sanity not always to be found in his contemporaries. It is perhaps symptomatic of the changed outlook that it is only possible to devote a comparatively short space in this study to Taylor's very detailed teaching on the subject.

It is in time of trouble, Taylor believes, that man's faith is proved: 'For in our health and clearer days it is easy to talk of putting trust in God; we readily trust Him for life, when we are in health; for provisions, when we have fair revenue; and for deliverance, when we are newly escaped: but let us come to sit upon the margent of our grave, and let a tyrant lean hard upon our fortunes and dwell upon our wrong, let the storm arise, and the keels toss till the cordage crack, or that all our hopes bulge under us, and descend into the hollowness of sad misfortunes, then can you believe, when you neither hear, nor see, nor feel anything but objections?'[1] Yet faith at such times reaps a rich harvest; God's strength is made perfect in our weakness. Furthermore, he says, God seldom punishes here and hereafter. Taylor, it would appear, tends to regard sickness as God's punishment of the backsliding Christian; for the vicious person, sickness is the beginning of God's vengeance.

Since he thought that fear of death might hinder the advantages of sickness, Taylor produces considerations and exercises to help Christians. While it is not a sin to be afraid, it is greater happiness to be free from fear — a felicity which our Lord denied Himself in Gethsemane. If, however, fear should prevent us from doing our duty or from being patient, we either love this world too much or do not trust God enough for the next. Patience, faith and repentance are to be practised by the sick. The first of these is, of course, a part of fortitude. 'Do not think that God is only to be found in a great prayer, or a solemn office: He is moved by a sigh, by a groan, by an act of love.'[2] This implies patience in the desires of religion. As he says rather bluntly, 'Be content, that the time, which was formerly spent in prayer, be now spent in vomiting . . .' This patience must be expressed also in our relationships with others. Doctors must be obeyed in matters that concern them, though we are not to place too much confidence in them 'or drain our hopes of recovery from the fountain through so imperfect channels'.[3] Servants and nurses should be treated kindly: 'Remember, that thou art very troublesome to them; that they trouble not thee willingly.'

Concerning faith, Taylor recommends that it should be specially active about the promises of grace, and that the recital of the Creed should be mingled with the patient's prayers. Faith ought to be turned into a love of the Articles. 'An act of love will make him have a mind to it; and we easily believe what we love.'[4] With regard to repentance,

---

[1] *Works*, III, p. 328.   [2] *ibid.*, p. 357.   [3] *ibid.*, p. 357.
[4] *ibid.*, p. 367.

K

the invalid is to repent of any sin which may be connected with the cause of sickness. General sorrow for sin, recalling past confessions and restitution where necessary are all aids. The sick man should consider God's goodness and justice in His punishments, praying frequently and submitting patiently to the rod of sickness and doing some great act of charity. In any other matter he is to take the advice of a spiritual guide.

We have attempted in this section to let Taylor speak for himself on a number of subjects connected with the development of Christian character as displayed in the exercise of prudence, temperance and fortitude. It hardly needs reiterating that it is impossible to sustain the divisions all the way, and it is unlikely that they would have the unqualified assent of all moral theologians. They do, however, provide a framework and into whatever categories we place these virtues, they form a necessary part of Christian character.

If Taylor's attitude to temperance in all its aspects seems trivial at times, we may remind ourselves that detailed guidance was probably necessary for some of his readers and that not all of his conclusions are arrived at by common sense to-day. If his fortitude strikes us as of a rather passive kind, and we feel that there is in it little of the faith of the martyrs or the courage of those who preferred to suffer rather than forego their principles, we ought to remember that Taylor himself endured a good deal because of his strongly held convictions. If it is suggested that there are occasions when he seems to defer to the customs of his hosts, it must not be forgotten that in his life as a whole, and particularly in his later years in Ireland, he did not shrink from decisions that led to unpopularity.

3. THE CHRISTIAN IN SOCIETY

In examining Taylor's teaching about the behaviour of the Christian in society, we shall consider it, as he does, in connection with the cardinal virtue of justice. This virtue, no less than the others, has been interpreted in various ways, but perhaps more than any of the others its meaning has changed with the climate of opinion. The word 'righteously' from the Epistle to Titus which Taylor is expounding does not help, because the non-Christian may use that word in a general sense which is exclusive of any Christian content.

To define justice as synonymous with law does not go far enough, nor for the Christian may it be comprehended in the phrase 'rendering to everyone his due'. Christian righteousness exceeds that of the Pharisees and follows the example of the God Who sends his rain on the just and unjust. Christian justice might therefore be summed up more adequately in the command to love our neighbours as ourselves, remembering that this is a love which springs out of our love of God and His love of us. In other words it exceeds what is commonly understood by philanthropy. It is hardly necessary to add that because justice affects our relations with other people, it is quite impossible to try to link it with one aspect of experience; thought, feelings and will are all involved.

Taylor distinguishes between two kinds of justice. The first is commutative and concerns negotiations and restitution; the second is distributive and deals with obedience and provision. In writing of the former, Taylor uses the words of our Lord: 'Whatsoever ye would that men should do to you, even so do to them.' In his explanation Taylor stresses the importance of a *quid pro quo* rather than the words 'Whatsoever ye would', but we see the relevance of his interpretation in connection with fair exchange in the economic sphere. In distributive justice, that is man's responsibility to society, Taylor quotes St Paul: 'Render to all their dues . . . Owe no man anything but to love one another.' This principle is not concerned with economic exchange but 'passes upon us by virtue of some command of God or of our superior, by nature or by grace, by piety or religion, by trust or by office'.[1] Commutative justice then

[1] *Works*, III, p. 115.

applies to equals with regard to contracts; distributive justice deals with the respective duties of each person in his own sphere — master and servant, father and children and other relationships of this kind. Strictly speaking, according to Taylor, we should exclude from a definition of justice the obedience which we owe to our superiors; this is a part of piety and religion: 'For as he is not called a just father who educates his children well, but pious; so that prince who defends and well rules his people, is religious, and does that duty for which alone he is answerable to God.'[1] It will be seen that this conception differs from that which is held by many Christians to-day. The rise of democracy has brought with it a governmental responsibility to the electors which is far removed from Taylor's concept.

With this introduction in mind, we may begin by seeing how Taylor views the Christian in relation to the state. We have noted already his strong belief in authority and in the duty of the Christian to obey.[2] There is much in his teaching which is reminiscent of the hymn: 'I vow to thee my country' and in particular the line 'The love which asks no questions.' The duty of the ruler to his subject implies the promulgation of laws for the defence of property, the encouragement of labour, for safety, for settling controversy, for recording noble actions and for promoting trade. Severity is to be 'tempered with dispensations, pardons and remissions', and under the guidance of the ruler the law is so to be administered that it helps rather than hinders. Rulers are to be the guardian of pupils and widows. The law should be simple, trials fair, and it should not be possible to buy the office of a judge. In granting pardons the end of justice must be served; the injured party should be given satisfaction, lest indulgence makes the people bold to do wrong.[3]

The duty of authority is summed up elsewhere in his writings: 'Christian parliaments must exceed the religion and

---

[1] *Works*, III, p. 119.
[2] See above on Law, p. 53; also II, p. 115 ff.; III, p. 116 ff.
[3] *ibid.*, p. 123 ff.

government of the *Sanhedrin*. Your laws must be more holy, the condition of the subjects be made more tolerable, the laws of Christ must be strictly enforced, you must not suffer your great Master to be dishonoured, nor His religion dismembered by sects, or disgraced by impiety: you must give no impunity to vicious persons, and you must take care that no great example be greatly corrupted; you must make better provision for your poor than they did, and take more care even of the external advantages of Christ's religion and His ministers, than they did of the priest and Levites; that is, in all things you must be more zealous to promote the kingdom of Christ, than they were for the ministries of Moses.'[1]

In spite of the emphasis on the authority of the state at the expense of the individual, which would not commend itself to Christians to-day, it is good to note that Taylor does not neglect the responsibility of the supreme power towards the people. A modern manual of moral theology would cover a very much wider field than was envisaged by Taylor in his writings, but this is not surprising when we remember the changes which have taken place. We ought to take note of the fact that Taylor is anxious that Christian principles should be applied to both government and governed, and recognize that however dated his views may be, his piety included a serious consideration of political thought.

In writing of the Christian duty of obedience, Taylor includes, as we should expect, a section on the acceptance of ecclesiastical authority. The ground has been covered in the section on Law; we may merely remark that Taylor stresses here the fact that while our duty to governors is based on 'Render to Caesar the things that are Caesar's', with regard to ecclesiastical rulers he cites: 'Obey them that have the rule over you, and submit yourselves; for they watch for your souls, as they that must give account.' There is no doubt that he is envisaging a submission to authority in the Church which would not commend itself to many Christians to-day.

[1] *ibid.*, VIII, p. 264.

In *Holy Living* there is no account of the duties of the Church to its members. 'The duty of ministers and spiritual guides to the people', says Taylor, 'is of so great burden, so various rules, so intricate and busy caution that it requires a distinct tractate by itself.'[1] One has only to glance at a list of Taylor's works to see how he sought to fulfil the duty of the Church to feed the sheep and care for the lambs of the flock. His own insistence on the value of spiritual guides and the importance of the means of grace show clearly his desire to perfect men in holiness. More than this he provided means, particularly in *Holy Living* and *Holy Dying*, *Unum Necessarium* and *Ductor Dubitantium*, to give help to those who were to be spiritual counsellors. His sermon on 'The Whole Duty of the Clergy' and his *Rules and Advices*, the latter designed for the clergy of the diocese of Down and Connor containing eighty-seven rules about 'their deportment in their personal and public capacities', all reveal a serious sense of responsibility. Both *Holy Dying* and his *Rules and Advices* contain suggestions about the visitation of the sick and dying. Whatever accusations can be levelled against the Church for neglecting its duty by way of provision, the charge can hardly be laid at Taylor's door.

The most important way, according to Taylor, in which the Church can discharge its duty is by an example of holiness in its ministers: 'A minister of an evil life cannot do so much good to his charges, he cannot profit them, he is not useful . . . a good sermon without a good example, is no very good sermon.'[2] 'He that lives an idle life may preach with truth and reason, or as did the pharisees; but not as Christ or as one having authority.' Again, 'If your charges see you bear your sickness patiently, and your cross nobly, and despise money generously, and forgive your enemy bravely, and relieve the poor charitably; then he sees your doctrine is tangible and material, it is more than words, and he loves you, and considers what you say.' Patience, constancy, courage and Christian magnanimity in the

---

[1] *Works*, III, p. 130.   [2] *ibid.*, VIII, p. 509.

minister will enable him to help his people in their difficulties.[1]

The minister is to be prudent but he is not to allow respect
of persons, public opinion or even criticism to deflect him
from his duty. On the other hand, he is not to indulge in
chidings, intemperate talking and sudden and violent
expressions: 'If you cheaply and lightly be engaged upon
such low usages with any person, that person is likely to be
lost from all possibility of receiving much good from your
ministry.' In Taylor's day, as is common knowledge, the
clergy had a good deal of authority. This, he urges, is to be
used for the benefit of the weak as well as the strong: 'Suffer
no houses of debauchery, of drunkenness or lust in your
parishes; but implore the assistance of authority for the
suppressing of all such meeting-places and nurseries of
impiety; and as for places of public entertainment, take care
that they obey the rules of christian piety, and the allowed
measures of the law.' In dealing with divisions, Taylor urges
firmness, but piety is to be judged by faith, obedience to the
law and love to Christian people, rather than by options.
Zeal is to be guided into useful channels. The unlearned are
to be encouraged to express their faith in deeds rather than
words. 'Never appeal to the judgement of the people in
matters of controversy; teach them obedience, not arrogancy;
teach them to be humble, not crafty.' The permitted
ceremonies of the Church are to be explained to the congregation.[2]

We have already referred to Taylor's emphasis on the
importance of preaching. The wise counsel in his *Rules and
Advices* is aimed at building up Christian character. He urges
ministers to instruct young people in the catechism, but
older ones who are ignorant of the faith are to be present on
these occasions, 'that no person in your parish be ignorant
in the foundations of religion.' Parishioners are to be taught
the benefits of mental prayer, meditation and confession. All
the needs of the soul are to be met through preaching,

[1] *ibid.*, I, p. 100 ff.   [2] *ibid.*, p. 105 f.

teaching and personal guidance. Ministers are to be faithful in visiting the sick, not waiting to be sent for; in trying to answer the problems of such persons, they must not consider who they are but what questions they ask. Taylor concludes his advices by stressing the importance of the sacraments, public prayers, the care of the poor and guiding the people.[1]

Though we have looked at the subject of the duty of the Church from the standpoint of Taylor's emphasis on the responsibility of the clergy, a picture emerges of what the Church ought to do for those for whom it must care. The situation differs today in that many a parish priest, unlike his predecessors, cannot know every person for whom he has spiritual responsibility. In those days clerical authority depended not only on tradition but on the layman's general lack of education. The idea of lay responsibility in Church government was unknown in the way it is today. Nevertheless, within the limits in which he writes, Taylor's views are of importance.

In considering the Christian in society, we must look at Taylor's teaching under two heads: the first is concerned with his business transactions and the second with more personal relationships. In negotiations and civil contracts Taylor says that our duty is plain: honesty, sincerity, simplicity and faithfulness are all required. He goes carefully into the meaning of justice as it is to be applied to business dealings.[2] In bargains there must be freedom from any sort of deceit, not merely abstention from falsehood. With this caution in mind, it is lawful to buy as cheaply as possible and to sell as dear as we can; this, however, concerns dealings between equals, for example merchants with merchants and rich with rich. Monopoly or necessity is not to influence the price; it is to be what is generally accepted as reasonable. It is not right to try to gain the maximum profit lest we should be tempted to go beyond it in the future.

With proper safeguards, Taylor is prepared to allow a higher price to be charged if the seller is not to receive

---

[1] *Works*, I, p. 111 f.   [2] *ibid.*, III, p. 130 ff.

payment at once. In this, he and other casuists of the seventeenth century depart from Aquinas who regarded such a course as coming under the forbidden practice of usury. Taylor, in a letter to John Evelyn, agreed that it is permissible to charge interest on a loan so long as it does not exceed what is lawful, for he believes that the money entrusted to us by God is to be used for the benefit of dependents.[1]

There is to be no raising of rents or prices because of a man's person; a prince is to be treated as justly as a beggar, though in the case of the latter we must be sure to see that justice is tempered with mercy. A poor man must not make his poverty an excuse for driving a hard bargain. The hired servant is to be paid his wages promptly, 'according to covenant or according to his needs.' However much it may be to our disadvantage, we are to keep our promises. No man may take money for that which he cannot do; doctors are not to accept the incurable as patients without first saying that there is no hope; advocates must tell their clients of the true dangers of their case. What God has given to all must not be seized by one person for his private property.

In writing of restitution, Taylor distinguishes between the transient act of sin against God and the evil which remains. He quotes from Augustine: 'Our sin can never be pardoned till we have restored what we unjustly took, or wrongfully detain.' Taylor adds: 'Restored it, I mean, actually or in purpose and desire, which we must really perform when we can.'[2] In writing of the rules for making restitution, Taylor includes as guilty all who are accessories to a wrong act. If a greater evil results than was intended, then reparation must be made for all that actually happened. If the act of almsgiving has been hindered through force or fraud, not simply by discouragement, then restitution is necessary. Money accepted as a bribe or a forfeit taken from a neighbour without legal sanction must be restored. Restitution is

[1] H. B. Wheatley, *Diary and Correspondence of John Evelyn*, III, p. 249.
[2] *Works*, III, p. 134.

not incumbent on an heir in personal matters but only if the estate is involved.

To injure one's neighbour demands restitution, though Taylor draws a distinction in the case of adultery between enticement with willing consent and consent because of deceit or violence. The adulterer must make reparation by supporting if necessary any illegitimate children. The man who kills another must look after the widow and children. Restitution must be made by the man who through fraud or violence takes away the reputation of his neighbour. Financial reparation must be made by the man who injures his neighbour in such a way as to make him incapable of working, and this rule applies to false imprisonment. The person who is unable to estimate how many he has defrauded ought to give to the poor what he has taken deceitfully. If restitution does not come within the law of the land, we are to settle it by the necessity of the creditor, the time of delay and the special obligations of friendship or kindness.

There is another sort of restitution: the obligation of friendship and returning good for good: 'Our duty to our benefactors is to esteem and love their persons; to make them proportionable returns of service or duty, or profit, according as we can, or as they need, or as opportunity presents itself, and according to the greatness of their kindness, and to pray to God to make them recompense for all the good they have done to us; which last office is also requisite to be done for our creditors, who in charity have relieved our wants.'[1]

In turning to personal relationships, we are going beyond justice in its narrowest sense but not beyond the Golden Rule which Taylor applies to our dealings with our fellows in civil contracts. Some of these aspects, such as the works of mercy included in almsgiving, we have already taken note of as being mixed acts of religion.

Since we have just been considering Taylor's teaching about restitution, we may well look at what he has to say

[1] *Works*, III, p. 139.

about the attitude of the injured party. Though, as we have seen, he does not believe it right to defend our lives against an angry or unjust prince, he allows the use of all artifices to avoid death; if it is necessary to kill in order to preserve our lives it is not to be done in a vengeful spirit.[1] But Taylor has no sympathy with duels in defence of honour. So often honour is 'nothing but a reputation amongst persons vain, unchristian in their deportment, empty and ignorant souls, who count that the standard of honour which is the instrument of reprobation; as if to be a gentleman were to be no Christian.'[2] Taylor is not happy either about Christians going to law: he has little faith in its processes. It is allowable in 'defending of widows and orphans, and churches, which in estimation of law, are, by way of fiction, reckoned to be in pupilage and minority; and also respecting our own interests, when our necessities, and the support of our family and relatives require it: for all these are cases of charity and duty respectively'.[3]

Elsewhere Taylor emphasizes the necessity of forgiving so as to forget. A man may be God's enemy; we are not to make him ours. There are two kinds of forgiveness: pardon and restitution to friendship. We are to seek both, though we are not bound to trust our friend in the particular instance in which he failed: 'No charity ties thee to be a fool.'[4] How long and how often are we to forgive? The measure of Christ is to be ours; we are to consider our own need of forgiveness and forgive our brother as often as he sins. We are not to demand mathematical demonstrations of genuineness: 'Let every good act be forwardly entertained, and persuade you heartily that all is well within.' After the second and third relapse, we are not bound to accept the offender's statement that he has repented, nor after a thousand injuries can he expect to be employed or returned to all his former capacities of good. Some signs of repentance we must accept: open confession of the fault, with

[1] ibid., II, p. 450.   [2] ibid., p. 450 f. See also X, p. 140.
[3] ibid., II, p. 457. See also X, p. 144.   [4] ibid., VIII, p. 135.

circumstances of shame and dishonour; on oath; the signs used before God when employed before men. 'To the question Whether of the parties must begin the peace; I answer, that both are bound . . . . If the criminal does not come, the offended person must offer peace; he must go or send to him.'[1]

Another aspect of the way in which the Christian conducts himself in society concerns speech. Taylor has little hope that the talkative person may be cured, though he advises writing as a possible means of dealing with this fault. He includes as vain talking: speaking like a fool, foolish jesting and revealing secrets.[2] The use of oaths, unless made to God or His vice-gerent, is forbidden, though this does not include assertory oaths. Taylor, as we should expect, is opposed to what he calls 'that low, cheap, unreasonable, and inexcusable vice of customary swearing'.[3] He is severe on those who use vile language to a servant who has made a foolish mistake.[4] In criticizing slander and flattery, he speaks of the latter as the worst way of misusing speech. To flatter by underestimating the gravity of a sin is to encourage it. But not all praise is flattery: 'It may nourish up an infant virtue and make it grow up towards perfection, and its proper measures and rewards.'[5]

The Christian in his life in society has a responsibility to his weaker brother.[6] Not everything that might be considered to be a stumbling-block is to be abjured; all religion has been abused by some who are over-scrupulous. Peevish people, he says, are not to betray the liberty given us by Christ. Yet it is possible for our example to give offence and this is scandal. Our responsibility for others means that we may have to question the ways by which men obtain a living. Those who are employed in what he calls arts and trades which minister to trifling pleasures (jugglers, tumblers, players, fencers and the like) do these things because they are uneducated. Were they more learned they would be better employed. Spiritual guides should try to help them to this.[7]

---

[1] *Works*, VIII, p. 140.   [2] *ibid.*, IV, p. 273 ff.   [3] *ibid.*, II, p. 428.
[4] *ibid.*, IV, p. 300 f.   [5] *ibid.*, p. 305 f.   [6] *ibid.*, II, p. 572.
[7] *ibid.*, X, p. 585.

This question of employment raises the issue of what recreations are lawful for the Christian since the instruments for them have to be made. Taylor has some interesting observations on card-playing and dice. He admits the troubles which so frequently accompany such sports but believes that a good man may legitimately find recreation in them. He urges that there should be moderation and playing for relaxation rather than for money. He thinks that it may be legitimate to play for small sums; the trouble arises when large amounts are involved. He does not seem to see the possibility of those who start in a small way becoming absorbed in gambling, nor does he deal with the principle involved in gambling itself. Taylor does not approve of large sums being won, for even if the winnings are given away, 'what bounty is that by which I reward my friends and servants with another man's estate?'[1] Young people (who have great passions, fierce desires and quick angers) should not be allowed to play. Some words of Taylor's, written originally about card-playing, may be taken in a wider context: 'We must neither do evil, nor seem to do evil: we must not converse with evil persons, nor use our liberty to our brother's prejudice or grief: we must not do any thing which he with probability or with innocent weakness thinks to be amiss, until he be instructed rightly; and if he be, yet if he will be an adversary, and apt to take opportunities to reproach you, we must give him no occasion.'[2]

It will be obvious that we have had to pass over many aspects of the life of the Christian in society in selecting the few that we have dealt with here. We do, however, gain an impression of Taylor's general outlook. It is the character of the Christian that absorbs him and, though he gave detailed guidance on many aspects of the Christian's life and work in relation to his fellows, his general attitude may be summed up in the words: 'This world would be an image of heaven, if all men were charitable, peaceable, just and loving.'[3]

[1] ibid., X, p. 597.   [2] ibid., p. 601.   [3] ibid., II, p. 523.

Before we leave the subject of relationships we must turn
to what Taylor had to say about friendship. He was asked
by a Mrs Katherine Phillips, herself a writer, 'how far a dear
and perfect friendship is authorized by the principles of
Christianity?'[1] By friendship Taylor assumes his questioner to
mean 'the greatest love and the greatest usefulness, and the
most open communication, and the noblest sufferings, and the
most exemplar faithfulness, and the severest truth, and the
heartiest counsel, and the greatest union of minds of which
brave men and women are capable'. This, says Taylor, is
really Christian charity which is friendship to all the world.

There is nothing in Christianity against friendships; there
is only a danger that they should become too exclusive. This
is almost inevitable because we are limited ourselves through
nature and circumstances. The choice of friends, therefore,
is important and we ought to select them for their goodness:
'My friend is a worthy person when he can become to me
instead of God, a guide or a support, an eye or a hand; a
staff or a rule.'[2] There may be lesser attractions which 'first
strike the flint and kindle a spark' but a true friendship must
be built on something more solid. We are to love our friends
as we love ourselves but we must not therefore excuse their
sin; then it becomes a conspiracy not friendship. Family
relationships differ from friendship, though fraternal relations
provide a preliminary disposition: 'A brother does not
always make a friend, but a friend ever makes a brother
and more.'[3] Marriage is the queen of friendships.

With regard to friendships with members of the opposite
sex, Taylor says there is to be prudence and freedom from
suspicion, though when these cautions have been observed
scandalmongers are to be despised. He makes a particular
point of the capacity of women for noble friendship: 'A
woman can love as passionately, and converse as pleasantly,
and retain a secret as faithfully, and be useful in her proper
ministries.'[4] She is not so good a counsellor as a wise man

---

[1] *Works*, I, p. 71 ff.   [2] *ibid.*, p. 78.   [3] *ibid.*, p. 89.
[4] *ibid.*, p. 94.

nor as helpful in sorrow or in trouble but in peaceful times 'virtuous women are the beauties of society and the prettiness of friendship'. He concludes with ten rules for conducting friendships.

Taylor's statements, though perhaps rather academic in tone, are sane and sensible. If he says nothing original, he marks out the path clearly and avoids being either over-sentimental or too severe. It is a part of his interpretation of Christian piety that the conversation of friends, no less than devotional acts, should be crowned with the blessing of God.

Taylor could write with some experience on the subject of piety at home. As we have seen, he married twice and was the father of several children. He had also taught for a time in South Wales and the numerous allusions to children in his writings suggest that he was familiar with their ways.[1] In this section we must consider his attitude to marriage, parents, children, and refer briefly to his Catechism for the young.

Taylor has the highest view of what married life may be: 'Here is the proper scene of piety and patience, of the duty of parents and the charity of relatives; here kindness is spread abroad, and love is united and made firm as a centre: marriage is a nursery of heaven; the virgin sends prayers to God, but she carries but one soul to Him; but the state of marriage fills up the numbers of the elect, and hath in it the labour of love, and the delicacies of friendship, the blessing of society, and the union of hands and hearts; it hath in it less of beauty, but more of safety, than the single life; it hath more care, but less danger; it is more merry and more sad; is fuller of sorrows, and fuller of joys; it lies under more burdens, but it is supported by all the strengths of love and charity, and those burdens are delightful.'[2]

In writing of the mutual duties of husband and wife, Taylor urges particular care against unkindness in the early

[1] ibid., II, p. 207 f. 'He (Satan) hath apples to cozen children and gold for men.' 'If a man goes to his prayers as children go to school he will soon find excuse for omitting them.' (ibid., IV, p. 166). There are other examples.
[2] ibid., IV, p. 211. From a sermon on 'The Marriage Ring.'

days of marriage before it is stable enough to withstand disagreements. Husbands and wives are to avoid what is likely to upset the other, just as (Taylor adds rather quaintly) keepers of elephants never appear before them in white. Everything is to be shared. Each has obligations to the other: he rules her by authority and she rules him by love. Though Taylor believes in the superiority of men, he describes the functions of husband and wife in terms of *dominus* and *domina*, lord and lady, master and mistress. He points out that St Paul never says how husbands are to exact obedience; all their duty is summed up in loving their wives. The Christian husband will ease life for his wife, tolerating her infirmities and setting her a good example.[1]

Wives are to obey their husbands out of love. A woman is to a man as body is to soul: 'A woman can never become equal but by obeying.'[2] Compliant is the word which Taylor applies to the good wife: sweetness of manners, humble comportment, fair interpretation of all addresses, ready compliances, high opinion of him and mean of herself are to be preferred to cosmetics and gallantry in clothes and jewels. Taylor suggests that if a husband is morose, a good wife will ask herself: 'If while I do my duty my husband neglects me, what will he do if I neglect him?'[3] But though she is to be compliant, particularly in religious matters, she is not to follow her husband into evil; her affection for him is not to warp her judgement in moral decisions. She may help towards his conversion. He gives illustrations to prove his point.[4]

With his customary thoroughness, Taylor goes into the question of matrimonial chastity and stresses the danger of love being replaced by lust.[5] He has guidance to give also to the wife of an adulterous husband.[6] It is an act of piety and charity for her to cohabit with such a man. As Christ forgave the woman taken in adultery, so may the husband

---

[1] *Works*, IV, p. 225. See also VIII, p. 126. Fuller, *The Holy State and the Profane State* (p. 203 ff.), has similar views.
[2] *ibid.*, IV, p. 228.   [3] *ibid.*, III, p. 129.   [4] *ibid.*, IV, p. 530.
[5] *ibid.*, III, p. 62 ff.   [6] *ibid.*, IX, p. 240-6.

if the erring wife repents. There is no compulsion, and if the innocent party desires liberty there is no wrong in it. On the other hand the innocent party may retain the guilty simply on the grounds of love or to maintain temporal rights. This is to last as long as there is hope of repentance, even if there is no immediate prospect of success and all means are to be used to achieve this. In scandalous case, like the wife of a clergyman committing adultery, there is more to be said for putting her away as an example, though even in this case it is a matter of decency and fittingness and not indisputable necessity. If tolerance aggravates the situation divorce may be the best way out, so long as it does not mean the opportunity for further indulgence in evil.

In his picture of the ideal marriage Taylor strikes a lyrical note: 'When a man dwells in love, then the breasts of his wife are pleasant as the droppings upon the hill of Hermon, her eyes are fair as the light of heaven, she is a fountain sealed, and he can quench his thirst, and ease his care, and lay his sorrows down upon her lap, and can retire home as to his sanctuary and refectory, and his gardens of sweetness and chaste refreshments.'[1]

Of the authority of fathers and the duty of the children to honour and obey them we have already seen Taylor's attitude. We may turn therefore to the responsibility of parents in the upbringing of their children. Parents will express their duty in different ways: 'A mother signifies her love one way, and a father another: she by fondness and tender usages, he by severe counsels and wise education.'[2] But fathers are not to provoke their children to wrath; they are to be pitiful, tender-hearted and gentle, teaching them according to their age: 'Secure their religion; season their younger years with prudent and pious principles; make them in love with virtue; and make them habitually so, before they come to choose or to discern good from evil, that their choice may be with less difficulty and danger: for while they are under discipline, they suck in all that they are first

[1] *ibid.*, IV, p. 224.   [2] *ibid.*, X, p. 67. See also III, p. 329.

L

taught, and believe it infinitely. Provide for them wise, learned, and virtuous tutors, and good company and discipline, seasonable baptism, catechism, and confirmation.'[1]

A good example of piety is to be set and such love shown to the children that they will look upon their parents as friends, patrons, defence, sanctuary, treasure and guide. Parents are to see that they are educated, 'and if we can without sin improve our estates for them, that also is part of the duty we owe to God for them.'[2] Parents are to provide husbands and wives for them, being certain first of the suitability from every standpoint of the interested parties.

Fathers have a special responsibility. The contented Christian man lives sweetly with his wife, affectionately with his children, providently and discreetly with his servants. 'But look upon a person angry, peaceless and disturbed; when he enters upon his threshold it gives an alarm to his house, and puts them to flight, or upon their defence; and the wife reckons the joy of her day is done, when he returns; and the children enquire into their father's age, and think his life tedious; and the servants curse privately, and do their service as slaves do, only when they dare not do otherwise.'[3] The father's responsibility is all the greater because his children are bound to him by special ties. If God smites them it is to punish him.

Taylor refers to the particular responsibilities of mothers. There were some women of the seventeenth century who handed over their children to nurses. Taylor cites the Virgin Mary as a contrary example.[4] Nurses, he says, can never have the same sense of responsibility as mothers and to leave children to them is to run the risk that ultimately nurses take the place of mothers in influence and affection.

Though the following words were actually addressed to the clergy, they are in keeping with Taylor's general ideas of how children should be brought up by their parents: 'A

[1] *Works*, III, p. 126. See also VII, p. 291.   [2] *ibid.*, p. 127.
[3] *ibid.*, II, p. 522 f.
[4] *ibid.*, II, p. 72-81. See also III, p. 13, and his tribute to Lady Carbery as a mother, VIII, p. 444 f.

little thing will fill a child's head; teach them to say their prayers, tell them the stories of the life and death of Christ, cause them to love the holy Jesus with their first love, make them afraid of a sin; let the principles which God hath planted in their very creation, the natural principles of justice and truth, of honesty and thankfulness, of simplicity and obedience, be brought into act and habit, and confirmation by holy sermons of the gospel. If the guides of our people would have their people holy, let them teach holiness to their children, and then they will, at least, have a new generation unto God, better than this wherein we now live.'[1]

There are prayers for the family, husband, wife and children and forms for morning and evening prayer scattered throughout Taylor's *Works*.[2] The best monument to his beliefs about the religious training of the young is to be found in *Golden Grove* which is an enlarged form of *A Catechism for Children* which had appeared earlier. In this work Taylor includes a compendium of what to believe and what to do. The title at the top of the page which follows the preface is: 'The Guide of Infant Devotion. Composed for the use of the devout, especially of younger persons.' The first part is entitled: 'A Short Catechism for the institution of young persons in the Christian religion.' There are forty-one questions and answers. Every answer has footnote references to passages in the Bible on which the answer is based. The next section in simple language expands the Apostles' Creed. The second part is entitled: 'Things to be done.' There are thirty-two rules, some of which are obviously not intended for children. This is followed by a manual of prayers for each day of the week (called *Via Pacis*) which leans heavily on Thomas à Kempis. Next follows a list of things to be prayed for which is really an exposition of the Lord's Prayer. Liturgies follow and the last section contains festival hymns. These hymns have never been used by the Church; many are unsuitable from the point of view of metre for congregational use.

[1] *ibid.*, V, p. 666. [2] *ibid.*, III, pp. 32 f., 112, 246; VII, pp. 297, 611 ff.

Though some of the subjects of *Golden Grove* are outside the scope of this chapter, light is thrown by the book on Taylor's real interest in children. In contrast to some Puritans who believed in reading the Bible through from beginning to end, Taylor says: 'Let it not be of the whole Bible in order, but for your devotion use the New Testament, and such portions of the Old as contain the precepts of holy life.' The historical and 'less useful part' can be read at other times.[1] There was and is a temptation to regard children as capable of adult experiences. In this connection Taylor is probably less of a sinner than others of his age. No doubt some modern educationists would consider him too severe in his approach; his own temperament was such as to suggest that he was a kindly father.

As in the State and Church, great changes have taken place in home life in the past three hundred years. The emancipation of women, including the altered attitude to the authority of husband over wife make some of Taylor's statement seem outmoded. If we cannot always accept his judgements on this subject, his general advice about the duties of parenthood are sensible and he presents a picture of a happy home which must have been drawn from his own experience. We can be thankful for the generally optimistic view of children held by Taylor: this is not the least of his attractions for a later age.

[1] *Works*, VII, p. 612 f. cp. Sandford Fleming, *Children and Puritanism*, p. 79.

CONCLUSION

◆◆◆

In the preceding pages we have examined Taylor's general theological position and have seen how he envisaged Christian piety both in theory and practice. We must now draw the threads together and ask how far he may be regarded as representative of any particular school of thought.

It will have been obvious from our study that Taylor was a man of his age who had his fair share of human failings. There is evidence in his writings to support Chillingworth's suggestion that Taylor slighted the arguments of his opponents; a good example of this is to be found in some of his criticisms of the Roman Church, where he is sometimes guilty of arguing from the particular to the general. There are instances when he may be accused with justice of special pleading, of using his sources uncritically, and of expressing views which his arguments could not sustain. His controversial writings particularly provide illustrations of his failure in these directions. Yet these shortcomings may be attributed to faults of temperament rather than of character. Taylor possessed the intuition of a poet rather than the logic of a philosopher. Having found an answer to a problem by intuition, his logic was not always able to support it. He was, by nature, a practical rather than a systematic theologian; his main interest lay in devotional not speculative divinity. In short, his conception of piety had a marked and increasing influence on his whole theological outlook.

We have noticed that the severest criticism was directed at Taylor because of his attitude to original sin and toleration. Yet he propounded his beliefs on both subjects out of a deep concern for holiness. In the case of the former doctrine, however unfortunately he expressed his views, Taylor's ideas sprang from a marked antipathy to the depersonalizing of sin and separating it from the sinner. He would have agreed with the writer of the *Apocalypse of Baruch* that 'each man has become the Adam of his own soul'. It was personal rather than racial responsibility which concerned Taylor for it was the individual whom he called to repentance. Connected with his interpretation of the doctrine was a growing conviction of the innocency of children who died in infancy, whom his charitable nature could not exclude from the love and mercy of God.[1]

This reference to Taylor's charity naturally leads us to think of his great work on toleration. It must be admitted that it was easier for a persecuted clergyman to preach toleration than for a harassed prelate to practise it; on this account Taylor has been charged with inconsistency. Yet the critics have sometimes failed to notice two factors to which particular attention has been drawn in this study. Taylor had to govern a diocese which contained uncompromising protagonists of the Presbyterian form of government, to which Taylor was opposed both by tradition and conviction. Secondly, in spite of the difficulties, we find echoes in the Irish period of the note sounded in *The Liberty of Prophesying*. If Taylor had written nothing else he would have put us in his debt, for this book is an impassioned plea for tolerance, that those who are united in their love for Christ should be united in their love for one another. Taylor's enthusiasm for holiness gave him a vision beyond that of ecclesiastical order, though his emphasis on the Apostles' Creed as a basis of agreement shows that his tolerance was born neither of apathy nor a lack of concern for doctrine.

There are other aspects of Taylor's teachings and writings which testify to his desire for a practical Christian piety. His orders of worship, the prayers which are scattered throughout his books, his cases of conscience and his emphasis on the

[1] See also Appendix for his letter to John Evelyn on this subject.

importance of spiritual guides all point in the same direction, though sometimes we may weary of his prolixity and question the relevance of some of the examples which illustrate his cases of conscience.

Is it possible to place Taylor in one particular category as as exponent of Christian piety? The limitations of such a course are obvious, but it may assist us if we make use of the framework of Mr R. H. Coats in his book *Types of English Piety*, where he distinguishes between the sacerdotal, the evangelical and the mystical. Mr Coats tells us that the sacerdotal type is represented by men like Hooker, Laud, Andrewes, Herbert and Nicholas Ferrar. Its strength lies in its historic appeal, its attraction for the sensuous imagination and its skill in enlisting all the arts in worship. It has, as its crowning act of worship, the Holy Eucharist. Its weakness lies in its tendency to pride, exclusiveness and rigidity; it may become the champion of the reactionary and of effete authority, and the foe of spiritual progress, civil and religious freedom and political reform. Christ's yoke may be made difficult and His burden heavy. In emphasizing the importance of forms and ceremonies, mint and cummin may be tithed but the weightier matters of the law neglected; enthusiasm and obedience may be lost in a multiplicity of ritual performances.[1] To express it in another way, religion may become something a man carries instead of something that carries him.

The glory of the evangelical type, according to Mr Coats, is in its stress upon the holiness of God, man's sin and the redemption wrought in Christ which enables the sinner to be saved by grace through faith. Men such as Milton, Baxter, and Bunyan are cited as its representatives. Its strength lies in its uncompromising attitude to man's needs, its simplicity, its emphasis on personal forgiveness and personal responsibility. It expresses itself in direct service to one's fellows and is the forerunner of social reform. It is weak on the corporate and institutional side and sometimes

[1] *op. cit.*, p. 9 ff., 244 f.

exaggerates man's depravity. It is inclined to narrow-mindedness and is antipathetic to culture in its broadest sense.[1]

The mystical type of piety finds expression in the works of men like Vaughan, Whichcote, Hales, More and George Fox. Mr Coats says: 'Mysticism, as a form of piety, is the passion and hunger of the soul for immediacy of access to the Father, and the all-satisfying vision of His eternal glory. 'Its chief characteristic is a kind of spiritual impatience with all that is merely mediate or imperfect in our knowledge of the Deity, and an ardour of desire to rise from the shadow to the substance, from illusion to reality, from the symbol to the thing symbolized, and to attain to the intoxicating blessedness of perfect union with the divine, so that self and the world shall be forgot in our absorption in the Father . . .'[2] Its strength is to save men from narrowness and sectarianism; it shows them the gleamings of the divine in what might be considered common and unclean. 'Its weakness is that it blurs the Christian outline and empties the historical revelation of its positive content.'[3] Mr Coats is careful to state that 'the truly characteristic experiences of the religious life are common to all types and specially confined to none'.[4] This means, of course, that we may expect to find saints in each type of piety. There will be overlapping; a sense of sin, for example, is not the prerogative of the evangelical type only.

On general grounds, Taylor would appear from the above analysis to be a representative of the sacerdotal type. His name can be mentioned without incongruity in the same breath as Andrewes and Laud. If it is suggested that he, unlike the others, produced ideas about original sin which led to accusations of Pelagianism, we can be sure that Taylor himself was never conscious of varying from the Creeds and Articles. Had he been regarded as completely heretical, it is most unlikely that he would have been offered

[1] *op. cit.*, p. 68 ff., 245 ff.   [2] *ibid.*, p. 156.   [3] *ibid.*, p. 248.
[4] *ibid.*, p. 257.

even an Irish bishopric. Yet if the sacerdotal type is synonymous with intolerance, Taylor's views, though strongly held
as we have seen, were moderated by his stress on the
importance of piety rather than opinion. Even the troubles
that befell him in his diocese did not prevent him from
retaining this distinction.[1]

In line too with the sacerdotal type of piety is Taylor's
emphasis on moral theology, in its broadest sense, and the
importance of spiritual guides. These are two aspects which
might well qualify him for condemnation as coming near
to that spiritual tyranny which Mr Coats deprecates. It is
true that Taylor's views on law, conscience and casuistry
owe much to the Schoolmen, but he is not bound slavishly
to their ideas and in his views of the distinction between
mortal and venial sin and the value of attrition and contrition, he took a line which was completely different from that
of most Roman exponents. These differences sprang from a
deep desire for holiness; in his stress on the gravity of sin,
Taylor is not surpassed by any of the Puritans. If he is to
be criticized for an interest in the confessional which is
foreign to the Protestant temperament, we must remind
ourselves of his uncomplimentary references to confession in
the Roman Church and that the Anglican confessional at
that time was as concerned with practical guidance as with
the confession of sin. Spiritual guidance was not confined to
Anglicans or Roman Catholics; did not Bunyan obtain
great help from his own pastor as well as from his reading
of the Bible?

It cannot be denied that the danger of legalism is always
present in interpreting moral theology in terms of law,
conscience and repentance. Yet, though it would be perilous
to press the analogy too far, there is certainly a correspondence between these and the 'soberly, righteously and
godly' which we considered under the outworkings of
Taylor's principles of piety. Without pursuing the analogy,
we may be thankful that he is able to give detailed guidance

[1] *Works*, I, p. 99 ff.

to the Christian in terms of growth in grace no less than of obedience to law. While it is true that his teaching is often linked with rules, these are best regarded as indications of a methodical approach; in more than one instance he makes it clear that he is making suggestions rather than exacting a minute obedience. If there is a danger of legalism, it must be remembered that Taylor was well aware of the troubles of the over-scrupulous. The temptation is not one that is likely to hinder the modern Christian; he comes to his decisions more frequently by way of intuition rather than by a careful weighing of probabilities. If there is a danger of pharisaic legalism in the one, the other may lead to antinomian laxity.

In his interpretation of the doctrine of justification by faith, Taylor would seem to have more in common with the sacerdotal than the evangelical type of piety. This doctrine has been a bone of contention both before and since the seventeenth century. Taylor's remarks about it causing divisions of heart among the faithful may be illustrated from our own times.[1] Those who oppose the doctrine of justification by faith alone object to the idea of faith being interpreted in a sense which appears to be more limited than that used in the New Testament: 'It is easy to make it mean a kind of feeling. It may be regarded as a good work, or as assent to a creed. Then the doctrine of justification by faith alone is open to all the objections urged against it.'[2] The watchwords of one generation are always in danger of becoming the catchwords of the next. A doctrine must not be judged by those who pervert its true meaning. At the same time it must be realized that words themselves are capable of a variety of meanings, as Taylor pointed out with regard to the use in Scripture of terms like faith, works and justification. Those who press most strongly for salvation by faith alone do so because they seek to emphasize the futility of good work as meritorious. Yet they hasten to add that such faith is not alone, it is productive of those works which

[1] See *Catholicity* and *The Catholicity of Protestantism*.
[2] *The Catholicity of Protestantism*, p. 74.

unaided man can never produce, including the sanctification of the whole personality; unless there is this result, such faith is not true faith.[1]

In the case of Taylor's presentation of the doctrine, he deals with faith rather with justification. He never teaches justification by works for he had scant sympathy with penances, indulgences and absolutions. But he does seem to view justification as a process rather than an act of acquittal. This element was not lacking in Luther. 'Baptism thus "signifies two things — death and resurrection: that is, full and complete justification",' says Luther, referring to Romans 6:4 and then explains that this 'justification' though it begins here on earth, is finally completed only when we die.[2]

This stress on process rather than crisis arises ultimately, though perhaps it did not do so in Luther's case, from the cleavage between Calvinistic and Arminian view. To the Calvinist, who believed that salvation was a matter of election, the position was straightforward: the man who was elected was justified, saved eternally, and brought forth the fruits of repentance and faith in holiness. If he fell away it was because he had never been saved. To do justice to the Calvinists, it must be added that most of them lived godly lives and did all in their power to 'make their calling and election sure'. Long before the theory of Dialectical Materialism they learnt the art of co-operation with the inevitable. The emphasis in Calvin as in Luther lies on the grace of God: salvation is Theocentric.[3] Taylor was an Arminian,

[1] Richard Baxter speaking of accepting Christ as Saviour and Lord says: 'It is not only to acknowledge His sufferings, and accept of pardon and glory, but to acknowledge His sovereignty and submit to His government, and way of saving; and I take all this to be contained in justifying faith.' (*The Saints' Rest*, Vol. I, p. 107.) After exhorting men to be serious in seeking their everlasting rest he says he has urged earnestness 'partly, because many eminent men of late do judge, that to work or labour for life and salvation is mercenary, legal and dangerous; which doctrine (as I have said before) were it by the owners reduced into practice, would undoubtedly damn them.' (*The Saints' Rest*, p. 266).

[2] P. S. Watson, *Let God be God!* p. 116.

[3] Richard Baxter gave much more space to assurance than Taylor did. See *The Saints' Rest*, Vols. I and II.

which meant, of course, that he envisaged the possibility of man falling away from grace. This, no less than Calvinism, presupposes the grace of God Who gives to man freedom of choice. But it also raises a problem: how far are works to be considered as necessary to salvation? If they are necessary, may it not tend to make salvation anthropocentric?

When we review what Taylor has to say on the subject it would seem to be a question of emphasis. Remembering those to whom he preached and the age in which he lived, is it not likely that he was giving needed correction about a doctrine which was liable to be abused? 'As he looked about him, he was appalled to see men lulled into an easy self-deception, knowing neither the gravity of sin nor the cost of Grace. He watched them being fobbed off with a cheap grace which touted the divine mercies, or saw them seeking to escape, by ascetic severities, a judgement in the light of which the most devoted sacrifice must appear trivial and irresponsible.'[1] These words were written about Martin Luther, yet with but slight modification they might be applied to Jeremy Taylor. For though watchwords change, human nature remains very much the same and the heart is all too prone to seek short cuts. It may be a formal reliance on the absolution of a priest, or a shallow repetition of some phrase about 'the blood of the Lamb'. At its best, each may mediate grace to the sincere sinner seeking reconciliation, but equally each may be used as a means to avoid the real issue of man's rebellion against the holiness of God.

It is pertinent to ask what affiliation, if any, Taylor has with the mystical type of piety. Dr Anderson Scott has defined what is usually meant by mysticism in these words: 'Mysticism as it developed in the Middle Ages stands for an experience of God which is sought by methods which become ever more elaborate, which call for the isolation of the individual, and the success of which usually represents the

[1] E. G. Rupp, *Studies in the Making of the English Protestant Tradition*, p. 164.

success of the individual rather than the success of God.'[1] Though Taylor is not unmindful of the mystic way, it would be a mistake to assume as some recent writers have done that he was attracted to mysticism in his later years.

In a biographical sketch, Miss Margaret Cropper has suggested that when Taylor went to Portmore he developed in the mystic way as he had not done before. She states that this period enabled him to finish his *Ductor Dubitantium*, and adds: 'But something else happened to Jeremy Taylor in this first Irish period, something that may well happen to anyone who goes into that country, where the things of the Spirit are so plainly shown in the lights and the shadows, the colours and shapes of every common day.'[2] She goes on to quote in support of her theory from a letter to Evelyn that Taylor wrote. 'I long, sir, to come to converse with you, for I promise myself that I may receive from you an excellent account of your progression in religion, and that you are entered into the experimental and secret way of it, which is the state of excellency whither good persons use to arrive after a state of repentance and caution. My retirement in this solitary place hath been, I hope, of some advantage to me as to this state of religion, in which I am yet but a novice, but by the goodness of God I see fine things before me whither I am contending. It is a great but a good work, and I beg of you to assist me with your prayers, and to obtain of God for me that I may arrive to that height of love and union with God, which is given to all those souls who are very deare to God.' Miss Cropper states that Bishop Heber thinks that there is something mystic in the tone that Taylor adopts in this letter, and she suggests that had he been left at Portmore, 'he might have produced a book of a different quality from *Holy Living*, or maybe he would have fallen silent before that which he discovered'.[3]

[1] *Living Issues in the New Testament*, p. 63 f. See also R. N. Flew, *The Idea of Perfection in Christian Theology*, esp. p. 151 ff. Heiler in his classic work on Prayer makes a similar distinction with regard to worship.
[2] M. Cropper, *Flame Touches Flame*, 142 f.
[3] *ibid.*, p. 143.

A little later, she returns to the same theme. Discussing Taylor's sermon at Dublin on 'If any man do His will, he shall know of the doctrine', she says: 'This same sermon takes us back to the Sally Island and Loch Beg, in its lovely description of a saint. This is a different note from any we shall find in *Holy Living*, something that Jeremy Taylor reached out towards in those quiet Irish mornings in the little summer house by the shining water.' She then quotes from Taylor's sermon: 'Lastly there is a sort of God's dear servants who walk in perfectness . . . and they have a degree of clarity and divine knowledge, more than we can discourse of, and more certain than demonstrations of geometry, and indeficient as the light of heaven . . . . But I shall say no more of this at this time, for this is to be felt not talked of; and they that never touched it with their finger may, secretly perhaps, laugh at it in their heart and be never the wiser. All that I shall now say of it is that a good man is united to God as a flame touches flame.'[1]

It looks at first sight as if Miss Cooper has made out a good case, and that Taylor was exploring the mystic way. But we must examine individually the points that she makes. It must be remembered first of all that in the sermon quoted Taylor was setting out the knowledge of doctrine that comes from obedience and not describing the unitive way to perfection, and when Taylor said obedience he meant action. This seems all the more clear from what has been said earlier in the sermon. He has stated that in every righteous man there is a new principle, the Spirit of Wisdom Who teaches us. 'Unless the Spirit of life be the informer of the spirit of man, the word of God will be as dead in the operation as the body in its powers and possibilities . . . Which principles divers fanaticks, both among us and in the Church of Rome, misunderstanding, look for new revelations, and expect to be conducted by ecstasy, and will not pray but in a transfiguration, and live upon raptures and extravagant

---

[1]M. Cropper, *Flame Touches Flame*, p. 150 f. A similar deduction is made by Mr Ross Williamson, *Jeremy Taylor*, p. 118 ff.

expectations, and separate themselves from the conversation of men by affectations, by new measures and singularities, and destroy order, and despise government, and live upon illiterate phantasms and ignorant discourses.'[1]

Miss Cropper reminds us that *Ductor Dubitantium* was completed at Portmore. This is what Taylor thinks of the mystic way (as recorded in that word) at the time when she imagines him to be pursuing it for himself. Advice to the scrupulous man contains this paragraph: 'The scrupulous man must avoid those companies, and those employments, and those books from whence the clouds arise, especially the books of ineffective and fantastic notion, such as are legends of saints, ridiculously and weakly invented, furnished out for ideas, not for actions of common life, with dreams and false propositions; for the scrupulous and fearful will easily be troubled, if they find themselves fall short of those fine images of virtue which some men describe, that they might make a fine picture, but like nobody. Such also are the books of mystical theology, which have in them the most high, the most troublesome, and the most mysterious nothings in the world, and little better than the effluxes of religious madness.'[2]

When dealing with the question of whether the service of God is to be preferred before anything else, Taylor says: '(It) is to be preferred before many things, but not before all things; not before many things of our ordinary life, not before many things of civil society. For to keep a holy-day is a part of the service of God, but not to be preferred before bodily labour in our trade, if that labour be necessary for the feeding of our family with daily bread. Contemplation is an excellent part of the divine service; but charitable actions are more useful. To hear a good sermon is good; but to snatch even an ox out of the pit is to be preferred before it. This our blessed Saviour taught us in those excellent words, "I will have mercy and not sacrifice." For not only the precise virtue of religion is the divine service, though by

[1] *Works*, VIII, p. 357 f.   [2] *ibid.*, IX, p. 275.

propriety it hath obtained the name: but the doing all our
duties, the works of our calling, all charitable ministries, all
useful trades, all graces of the Spirit expressed in actions
and obedience, is the service of God, and of one it cannot be
said, it is better than another; for they shall all be required
in their season.'[1] A little later he says: 'Ecstasies and raptures
and conversing with blessed spirits are certainly actions and
passions respectively of greater eminency than dressing the
sores of poor boys in hospitals; and yet he that does this
serves Christ and does good, while he that follows after the
others may fall into delusion of the devil.'[2] Again: 'Those
parts of the divine service which are most necessary, and do
most good to mankind, are to be chosen before those that
look more splendidly, and in themselves import more
perfection.'[3] In other words, Taylor sees a glory in the single
service of God, but recognizes that His service is to be found
also in the service of mankind. It certainly does not look as
if Taylor was as enthusiastic about the mystic way as Miss
Cropper would have us believe.

We know that Taylor was interested in Perfectionists while
he was in Ireland, for he asked Evelyn to find out more about
them, but we need not read too much into this enquiry.
There is a reference to Boehme in a letter to Evelyn. 'You
say right that they take in Jacob Behmen, but that is upon
another account, and they understand him as nurses doe
their children's imperfect language; something by use, and
much by fancy.'[4] The letter which Miss Cropper quotes is
commented on by Heber (Miss Cropper says 'nervously'):
'With such humility did the author of *Holy Living and Dying*
regard his own attainments in religion, and such were his
impressions of the happiness and consolation, even in this
life, conferred by a pure and exalted piety. If there is something mystic in the tone which he adopts, and we are
reminded, in spite of ourselves, of his previous inquiries
concerning the Perfectionists, let it be remembered that his

---

[1] *Works*, X, p. 227.   [2] *ibid.*   [3] *ibid.*, p. 228.
[4] Cited in *Works*, I, p. lxxxiv.

subsequent no less than his preceding writings bear testimony
to his freedom from any error of this kind . . . .'[1] It is worth
noting that Evelyn remarks in his diary, some years earlier,
that he went to hear Jeremy Taylor preach on the subject
of Evangelical Perfection. He later took him as his spiritual
adviser, so there is perhaps an added reason why they should
both be interested in this subject. We need not assume too
hastily that Taylor was a convert. Not everybody who
discussed in their letters the Oxford Movement (or the
Oxford Group Movement) could be written down as an
enthusiast.

It has been thought important to devote some space to
dealing with Miss Cropper's suggestions, for the piety of
Taylor is in the writer's view very far removed from that
mystical type of piety which has flourished from the Middle
Ages to our own time and is usually connected with the name
of Dionysius the Areopagite. It has been associated with
Origen whose general attitude was summed up in his
dictum: 'Contemplatives are in the house of God: those who
lead an active life are only in the vestibule.'[2] Taylor is more
in line with the writer who said: 'In the handiwork of their
craft is their prayer.'[3]

Taylor, of course, does not despise meditation, but he is
aware of the dangers of a contemplation that can lead to
'metaphysical and remote' considerations of God: 'Whenever
God's perfections be the matter of meditation', he says, 'we
should not ascend upwards into Him, but descend upon
ourselves, like fruitful vapours drawn up into a cloud,
descending speedily into a shower, that the effect of the
consideration be a design of good life. . . . The other kind of
love may deceive us.'[4] After describing the unitive way of
religion (some years before the sermon already quoted to the
University of Dublin) he warns his hearers that these visions
can often be illusions. He adds: 'It is more healthful and

---

[1] *ibid.*, I, p. lxxxviii.
[2] *Psalms*, 133. See also H. T. Hughes, *Prophetic Prayer*, p. 73 ff.
[3] *Ecclesiasticus* 38: 34.   [4] *ibid.*, II, p. 139.

M

nutritive to dig the earth and eat of her fruits, than to stare upon the greatest glories of the heavens and live upon the beams of the sun; so unsatisfying a thing is rapture and transportation to the soul; it often distracts the faculties, but seldom does advantage piety, and is full of danger in the greatest of its lustre.'[1] Of John the Baptist, he says: 'And yet after all these excellencies the Spirit of God called the Baptist forth to a more excellent ministry; for in solitude pious persons might go to heaven by the way of prayers and devotions, but in society they might go to heaven by the way of mercy, and charity, and dispensations to others.' Later he says that John and Jesus reconciled both ways. 'And from both we are taught, that solitude is a good school, and the world is the best theatre; the institution is best there, but the practice here; the wilderness hath the advantage of discipline, and society opportunities of perfection; privacy is best for devotion, and the public for charity. In both, God hath many saints and servants; and from both the devil hath had some.'[2]

The following passage is probably the one that would give most support to the mystical type of piety but we must note that it was written some years before Taylor went to Ireland, and it must be viewed in the light of his other statements. 'He that gives alms to the poor, takes Jesus by the hand; he that patiently endures injuries and affronts, helps Him to bear His cross; he that comforts his brother in affliction, gives an amiable kiss of peace to Jesus; he that bathes his own and his neighbour's sins in tears of penance and compassion, washes his master's feet; we lead Jesus into the recesses of our heart by holy meditations; and we enter into His heart, when we express Him in our actions.'[3]

Taylor calls men to the imitation of Christ's piety. 'His piety was even, constant, unblamable, complying with civil society, without affrightment of precedent, or prodigious instances of actions greater than the imitation of men. . . . The instances of His piety were actions of a very holy, but

[1] *Works*, II, p. 142.   [2] *ibid.*, p. 168 f.   [3] *ibid.*, p. 46.

of an ordinary life; and we may observe this difference in the
story of Jesus from ecclesiastical writings of certain beatified
persons, whose life is told rather to amaze us and create
scruples, than to lead us in the evenness and serenity of a
holy conscience.'[1] He would have men use the world and not
abuse it, using it 'for necessities of nature, and conveniences
of person, and discharge of all their duty and the offices of
religion, and charity to Christ and all Christ's members. . . .
He that hath all the world . . . enjoys the best part but in
common with the poorest man in the world'.[2]

In Taylor's opinion there are many delightful things that
are to be enjoyed. No one can read his works without being
impressed with his love of nature and his familiarity with it.
In a sermon on the text: 'Let us eat and drink, for tomorrow
we die' he points out that true felicity does not come from
the world, and that intemperance brings no happiness; but
he adds some rules to guide men so 'that nature and grace
may join to the constitution of man's felicity'.[3] 'It is lawful',
he tells us, 'when a man needs meat to choose the pleasanter,
even merely for their pleasures; that is, because they are
pleasant, besides that they are useful; this is as lawful as to
smell of a rose, or to lie in feathers, or change the posture of
our body in bed for ease, or to hear music, or to walk in
gardens rather than the highways; and God hath given us
leave to be delighted in those things which He made to that
purpose, that we may also be delighted in Him that gives
them.'[4]

We have seen already that Taylor has an attitude to
marriage far removed from those who regarded it as a
necessary evil. It is only necessary to give one additional
quotation: 'Celibate, like the fly in the heart of an apple,
dwells in a perpetual sweetness, but sits alone, and is confined
and dies in singularity; but marriage, like the useful bee,
builds a house and gathers sweetness from every flower, and
labours and unites into societies and republics, and sends

[1] *ibid.*, p. 41.   [2] *ibid.*, IV, p. 558.   [3] *ibid.*, p. 181.
[4] *ibid.*, p. 202.

out colonies, and feeds the world with delicacies, and obeys their king, and keeps order, and exercises many virtues, and promotes the interests of mankind . . . .'[1]

Another aspect of life may be taken to show that Taylor's piety was not other-worldly. After mentioning the dangers of jesting, he says more positively: 'The ecclesiastical history reports that many jests passed between St Anthony the father of hermits, and his scholar St Paul; and St Hilarion is reported to have been very pleasant, and of a facete, sweet, and more lively conversation; and indeed plaisance, and joy, and a lively spirit, and a pleasant conversation, and the innocent caresses of a charitable humanity is not forbidden.' Later he says: 'A cheerful spirit is the best convoy for religion.' And again: 'It is certain that all that which can innocently make a man cheerful, does also make him charitable . . . an amicable mirth can refresh the spirit . . . our heads may as well be anointed and look pleasant with wit and friendly entercourse, as with the fat of the balsam-tree; and such a conversation no wise man ever did, or ought to reprove. But when the jest hath teeth and nails biting and scratching our brother, when it is loose and wanton . . . then it is the drunkenness of the soul.'[2]

Enough has been stated to show that Taylor was a man who believed that all life belongs to God, and that every good thing can be welcomed as coming from Him. There is noticeable sometimes a tension which the late Dr W. R. Maltby has called 'the mastery of an unfavourable environment and the pressing of an alien thing into the service of God'.[3] Yet there is a definite advance on those who could see nothing of value in the material world. Taylor is averse from a piety absorbed in itself. As he says, in connection with obedience to God demanding different duties at various times: 'We must not be running after sermons when we should be labouring to provide meat for our family.'[4] Again,

---

[1] *Works*, IV, p. 211.   [2] *ibid.*, p. 291 f.
[3] W. R. Maltby, *The Significance of Jesus*, p. 68 f.
[4] *Works*, X, p. 63.

'The end of the mariner's art is not the salvation of the souls of them that sail with him, but the safe landing of their persons and goods at the port.'[1] A temporal end is part of our duty; and such are all the actions of our calling, whether our employment be religious or civil. Ploughman, artisan and marchant may serve God in their work as truly as king, priest and judge in their vocations.[2]

Dr Maltby, in the work already quoted, says: 'Sometimes it (the Church) has called men out of their secular employment in order to find God. More often it has accepted the common life as inevitable and urged men to discharge their part in it faithfully, but rather so as to be done with it than as rejoicing in it and looking to find a meaning of God in every part of it.'[3] Taylor, in the opinion of the present writer, does not come in the first category, and from the quotations given it seems that if he was not in the third type described by Dr Maltby, he was very near to it.

A final quotation may well close this section. 'And there is this excellency in all spiritual things, that they do not disadvantage to our persons, nor retard our just temporal interests: and the religion by which we carry Christ within us, is neither so peevish as to disturb our health, nor so sad as to discompose our just and modest cheerfulness, nor so prodigal as to force us to needs and ignoble trades; but recreates our body by the medicine of holy fastings and temperance, fills us full of serenities and complacencies by the sweetness of a holy conscience and joys spiritual, promotes our temporal interest, by the gains and increases of the rewards of charity, and by securing God's providence over us while we are in pursuit of the heavenly kingdom.'[4]

Though there are many references in Taylor's works to show that he saw time in the light of eternity, it is obvious from such works as *Holy Living* that his piety was of a practical nature and that he linked the whole of life with God. Dr

[1] *ibid.*, X, p. 232. See also II, p. 106. [2] *ibid.*, III, p. 8 ff.
[3] *The Significance of Jesus*, p. 69. [4] *Works*, II, p. 59.

McAdoo says that the outstanding feature of Caroline preaching in general is its universal interest in 'practical divinity'. There is, he says, no formalism, quietism or sentimentality in the Anglican devotion of the seventeenth century. It is thorough-going as to details, and thinks as much in terms of moral duty as spiritual graces. The Divine life in daily life might be its guiding maxim. 'But if it is much concerned with the pots and pipkins of religion, Caroline piety is not forgetful of the highest levels of spiritual life and labours to develop in men the faculty of seeing their daily conduct and devotional exercises in the light of their eternal destiny. "By their fruits ye shall know them" is written large across the manuals of the period.'[1]

In one sense Taylor makes no greatly original contribution to the practice of piety. Though he writes from a different standpoint, the sort of thing he was saying was being put forward by Richard Baxter whom we might define as a representative of the moderates and John Bunyan who is ecclesiastically poles apart from Taylor. Where all three meet is in their emphasis on the need for earnestness and sincerity in Christian living, in the practical directions that they give to help the disciple of Jesus to aim for holiness of life and in their evident devotion to Christ.

Bunyan's *Pilgrim's Progress* has outlasted both Baxter's *Saints' Everlasting Rest* and Taylor's *Holy Living and Holy Dying*, but without drawing detailed parallels between them it is obvious that the end of all three is the same; they are designed to guide the pilgrim in his journey to the Celestial City. Bunyan's work was the more vivid and picturesque, and it is probably to this fact more than to any higher standard that he set or better advice that he gave that his book has retained its popularity. Mr Douglas Bush's statement about Taylor's attitude might apply equally to all three: 'Life is a battle which at every moment, with God's aid or the devil's, we are winning or losing. By grace, repentance, and unceasing effort we are delivered alike from

[1] H. R. McAdoo, *The Structure of Caroline Moral Theology*, p. xi.

the old covenant and the bondage of sin into Christian liberty, love and joy.'[1]

Alongside this estimate of Taylor's attitude to life we may place a tribute to the man himself: 'He was no quiet churchman, living out a pleasant life among his books and in his garden, no placid saint whose halo gleamed in the sombre dark of a quiet cathedral. He was a warring soldier of the great church militant, a very mighty hunter before the Lord.'[2] Taylor knew and could appreciate books, gardens and the quiet cathedral atmosphere; he knew too the battlefield (literally and spiritually), wearisome controversy, persecution by his enemies and what it meant to struggle for the souls of men. Yet the main impression that we have of Taylor is of the shepherd, rather than the soldier or hunter. It would be hard to find anyone to whom the pastoral office meant more or who graced it with a greater devotion.

It is quite impossible to estimate how wide and great Taylor's influence has been, because his work touched the interior life of those who heard and read. We may assume that it has been far-reaching. There is some support for this assumption. Most people do not keep diaries or, if they do, their writings are not of sufficient importance to merit attention from subsequent generations. Two notable exceptions are John Evelyn and John Wesley. We know that each was profoundly influenced by Taylor, and we shall examine this influence more closely in the Appendix. We may regard them as 'straws' which indicate something of the way in which Taylor in his own and a subsequent age helped a growing circle. Up to the beginning of this century his *Holy Living and Holy Dying* was an inspiration to many. Of this work Dean Farrar said that only the *Theologica Germanica*, *The Imitation of Christ* and *Pilgrim's Progress* could compare in influence; 'and while this treatise equals them in sweetness and unction, in pathos and devotion, it far transcends them

---

[1] D. Bush, *English Literature in the Earlier Seventeenth Century*, p. 316.
[2] M. H. Nicholson, *Conway Letters*, p. 121.

in eloquence, imaginativeness and erudition.'[1] If this work is not widely read to-day, some of his prayers are still to be found in anthologies. As has already been stated, the new interest in moral theology has brought a revived interest in what Taylor had to say on this important subject.

In contrasting the sacerdotal and evangelical types of piety, Mr Coats states that they will produce two altogether different types of Christian saint. 'The one will give birth to the priest and the ascetic, the other to the prophet and reformer. The one will withdraw saintliness to the cloister, and cherish a clerical and retired holiness. The other will cultivate saintliness in homes, in senates, and in market-places, and produce some of its most shining examples of holiness from among the laity.'[2] Taken as it stands, it would certainly be doing an injustice to Taylor to place him in the sacerdotal type of piety outlined above. It may be admitted that he is not to be classed amongst the reformers of his age, and as a prophet he has more in common with his namesake than either an Amos or Isaiah. Nevertheless, he combined with his love of beauty and order a passionate desire that Christian piety should find its expression in the service of God and the service of man.

[1] *Masters in English Theology*, (ed. Dr A. Barry), p. 209.
[2] *Types of English Piety*, p. 97.

APPENDIX

The Influence of Jeremy Taylor on John Evelyn and John Wesley

INSCRIBED upon Evelyn's tomb are the words: 'There's no solid wisdom but in real piety.' It is no small tribute to Taylor if the help he gave to Evelyn resulted in such sentiments being associated with the diarist. A brief reference has been made already to the fact that after hearing Taylor preach, Evelyn took him as his 'ghostly father', to use his own description. He adds in his diary: 'I beseech God Almighty to make me ever mindful of, and thankful for, his heavenly assistances.'[1] Such correspondence between the two as has been preserved bears witness to the aid which Evelyn received from his spiritual guide.

Taylor could be frank as well as friendly and did not hesitate to remind Evelyn of the dangers attached to wealth and its appendages. He was also doubtful of the value of the time Evelyn devoted to his translation of Lucretius. He felt that the same pen ought to be employed in the glorification of God and in the ministries of eucharist and prayer.[2] His fears were allayed somewhat by Evelyn's reply to these charges and he wrote more happily about the 'pious annotation' which will save the reader from the snares of the pagan poet. Subsequent letters deal with a variety of topics, such as: the immortality of the soul, how God made everything out of nothing, the question of interest on loans, and perfection. Some reference has been made in earlier pages to these last two subjects.

[1] M. B. Wheatley, *Diary and Correspondence of John Evelyn*, II, p. 76. (The spelling has been modernized.)
[2] *ibid.*, III, p. 211.

One of the finest of Taylor's letters was written to Evelyn when the latter was bereaved by the loss of two sons. 'Your two boys are two bright stars, and their innocence is secured, and you shall never hear evil of them again. Their state is safe and heaven is given to them upon very easy terms; nothing but to be born and to die.' He urges Evelyn to comfort his wife by showing that 'you are more to her than ten sons'.[1]

With Taylor's removal to Ireland the correspondence became less regular and eventually lapsed, though there is reason to believe that the influence remained. It has been stated that amongst Evelyn's manuscripts was discovered one entitled *'Rules for using my pretious tyme well'*.[2] This it has now been decided belonged to his daughter Mary. There are a few marginal references from the Bible, Cosin, Patrick's *Devout Christianity*, *Agna genitalis* and *The Whole Duty of Man*, but none from Taylor.[3] John Evelyn, however, produced *A Devotionarie Book*. The book itself is not long and includes various helps in preparing for Holy Communion and receiving it spiritually, as well as a selection of short sayings which have obviously been gathered from several sources, though some are no doubt original to Evelyn. Two are given here which show a resemblance to Taylor, and he may have been responsible for others. The spelling has been modernized.

Evelyn: 'When a sin is dead and a habit crucified, 'tis then pardoned.'[4]

Taylor: 'No man's sins are pardoned, but in the same measure in which they are mortified, destroyed and taken away.'[5]

Evelyn: 'There is no repentance, but once taking it in a proper sense, seeing we are but once to change our state.'[6]

Taylor: 'For we must know that there is but one repentance in a man's whole life, if repentance be taken in the proper and strict evangelical covenant sense, and not after the

---

[1] *Diary and Correspondence of John Evelyn*, III, 245 ff.
[2] A. Ponsonby, *John Evelyn*, p. 130.
[3] I am indebted to Dr Geoffrey Keynes and Mr W. G. Hiscock, Deputy Librarian, Christ Church, Oxford, for help in this connection.
[4] *A Devotionarie Book of John Evelyn of Wotton*, (ed. W. H. Frere), p. 48.
[5] *Works*, VIII, p. 290.   [6] *op. cit.*, p. 49.

ordinary understanding of the word: that is, we are but once to change our whole state of life . . . .'[1]

* * *

Taylor's influence on John Wesley has probably been underestimated.[2] Methodism has rightly emphasized Wesley's experience in the room at Aldersgate on May 24th, 1738. Of this he wrote: 'I felt I did trust in Christ, Christ alone for salvation; and an assurance was given me that He had taken away *my* sins, even *mine*, and saved *me* from the law of sin and death.'[3] But the assurance which came to Wesley in 1738, which has such far-reaching results, was not the first crisis in his search for holiness. It began in 1725 and for this reason the 1738 experience has sometimes been called his 'evangelical conversion'.

When Wesley was first introduced to *Holy Living and Holy Dying* he was critical of parts of it, yet he wrote in 1777: 'In the year 1725, being in the twenty-third year of my age, I met with Bishop Taylor's *Rules and Exercises of Holy Living and Dying*. In reading several parts of this book I was exceedingly affected; that part in particular which relates to purity of intention. Instantly I resolved to dedicate all my life to God, all my thoughts, and words and actions; being thoroughly convinced, that there was no medium, but that every part of my life (not some only) must be either a sacrifice to God, or myself, that is, in effect, to the devil.'[4] As a result, Wesley planned a stricter life for himself and this led in the course of time to the Aldersgate Street experience in 1738. Between these dates he was influenced by the Moravians and gained much from them. But he was preserved from accepting faith to the exclusion of the rest of the commandments, he tells us, by English writers amongst whom he names Jeremy Taylor. Dr Rattenbury has suggested that in some ways the Moravians disappointed Wesley, and

---

[1] *Works*, III, p. 206.
[2] For a fuller account see the author's article ' Jeremy Taylor and John Wesley', *London Quarterly Review* (Epworth Press), October, 1949.
[3] *Journal of John Wesley*, I, p. 476.   [4] *Wesley's Works*, XII, p. 351.

he fell back on his earlier training. 'His own mind and character, trained in Laudian Anglicism, may be called the stuff which the Moravian experience set afire.'[1]

It has been stated that one immediate result of reading Taylor was the stricter life that Wesley formulated for himself. Perhaps it is possible to go further and say that Wesley's practice in later life of making rules sprang from his acquaintance with the writings of Jeremy Taylor. The later rules for a Helper, and the Societies, as has been pointed out by Simon, show dependence on Cave's *Primitive Christianity*, rather than Jeremy Taylor, though on many points the two are at one. However, a comparison of Wesley's *Diary* and Taylor's *Holy Living* show a very marked dependence on the latter; Wesley, even then, showed his genius for succinctness. In listing the parallels, considerations of space limit the quotations from Taylor.[2]

Wesley. 1: Begin and end every day with God; and sleep not immoderately.

Taylor. 1: In the morning when you awaken accustom yourself to think first upon God, or something in order to His service: and at night let Him close thine eyes: and let your sleep be necessary and healthful, nor be expensive of time . . . .

Wesley. 2: Be diligent in your calling.

Taylor. 2: Let every man that hath a calling be diligent in pursuance of its employment . . . .

Wesley. 3: Employ all spare hours in religion; as able.

Taylor. 3: Let all the intervals or void spaces of time be employed in prayers, reading, meditation . . . .

Wesley. 4: All holidays (holy-days).

Taylor. 4: The resting days of Christians, and festivals of the Church, must in no sense be days of idleness . . . but let them be spent in the works of the day, that is of religion and charity, according to the rules appointed.

Wesley. 5: Avoid drunkards and busybodies.

---

[1] *The Conversion of the Wesleys*, p. 17 ff.
[2] Wesley's rules are taken from his diary (*Journal* (Standard edition), I, p. 48-9), Taylor's rules from Vol. III, p. 10 ff.

Taylor. 5: Avoid the company of drunkards and busybodies . . .

Wesley. 6: Avoid curiosity, and all useless employments and knowledge.

Taylor. 14: Let every one of every condition avoid curiosity . . .
15: As much as may be, cut off all impertinent and useless employments of your life . . . .

Wesley. 7: Examine yourself every night.

Taylor. 22: In this we shall be much assisted . . . if before we sleep every night we examine the actions of the past day . . . .

Wesley. 8: Never on any account pass a day without setting aside at least an hour for devotion.

Taylor has several references to spending time every day in prayer.

Wesley. 9: Avoid all manner of passion.

Taylor devotes a whole section to chastity.

It is quite evident that there is dependence on Taylor in the rules that Wesley formulated with regard to the employment of his time: we shall see a similar indebtedness to Taylor in Wesley's rules as to intention.

Wesley. 1: In every action reflect upon your end.

Taylor. 1: In every action reflect upon your end . . . .

Wesley. 2: Begin every action in the name of the Father, the Son, and the Holy Ghost.

Taylor. 2: Begin every action in the name of the Father, of the Son, and of the Holy Ghost . . . .

Wesley. 3: Begin every important work with prayer . . . .

Taylor. 3: Let every action of concernment be begun with prayer . . . .

Wesley. 4: Do not leave off a duty because you are tempted in it.

Taylor. 8: If any temptation to spoil your purpose happens in a religious duty, do not presently omit the action, but rather strive to rectify your intention, and to mortify the temptation.

SELECT BIBLIOGRAPHY

P. Adair, *True Narrative of the Rise and Progress of the Presbyterian Church in Ireland*, (edited Killen), Belfast, 1866.

John Aubrey, *Lives*, (edited O. L. Dick), London, 1949.

A. Barry (editor), *Masters in English Theology*, London, 1877.

R. Baxter, *The Saints' Rest*, London, 1887.

W. J. Brown, *Jeremy Taylor*, London, 1925.

J. Bunyan, *Works*, (edited G. Offor), London, 1853.

D. Bush, *English Literature in the Earlier Seventeenth Century*, Oxford, 1945.

R. H. Coats, *Types of English Piety*, Edinburgh, 1912.

S. T. Coleridge, *Miscellanies*, London, 1911 edition.
Aids to Reflection, London, 1913 edition.

Horton Davies, *The Worship of the English Puritans*, London, 1948.

Dewar and Hudson, *Christian Morals*, London, 1948.

Gregory Dix, *The Theology of Confirmation in Relation to Baptism*, London, 1946.

C. H. Dodd, *Gospel and Law*, Cambridge, 1951.

C. W. Dugmore, *Eucharistic Doctrine in England from Hooker to Waterland*, London, 1942.

W. H. Fitchett, *Wesley and His Century*, London, 1906.

Sandford Fleming, *Children and Puritanism*, New Haven, U.S.A., 1933.

R. N. Flew, *The Idea of Perfection in Christian Theology*, Oxford, 1934.

W. H. Frere (editor), *A Devotionarie Book of John Evelyn of Wotton*, London, 1936.

T. Fuller, *The Holy State and the Profane State*, London, 1841 edition.

E. Gosse, *Jeremy Taylor*, London, 1903.

F. Greeves, *The Meaning of Sin*, London, 1956.

W. Haller, *The Rise of Puritanism*, New York, 1938.

F. Heiler, *Prayer*, London, 1932.

H. Henson, *English Religion in the Seventeenth Century*, London, 1903.
The Church of England, Cambridge, 1939.

R. Hooker, *Laws of Ecclesiastical Policy*, London, 1907.

H. T. Hughes, *Prophetic Prayer*, London, 1947.

W. K. Jordan, *The Development of Religious Toleration in England*, 4 vols., London, 1932-40.

K. E. Kirk, *Conscience and its Problems*, London, 1948 (revised edition).

 Some Principles of Moral Theology, London, 1921.

A. J. Macdonald (editor), *The Evangelical Doctrine of Holy Communion*, Cambridge, 1930.

W. R. Maltby, *The Significance of Jesus*, London, 1948.

H. R. McAdoo, *The Structure of Caroline Moral Theology*, London, 1949.

More and Cross (editors), *Anglicanism*, London, 1935.

I. Morgan, *The Nonconformity of Richard Baxter*, London, 1946.

R. C. Mortimer, *The Elements of Moral Theology*, London, 1953.

M. H. Nicholson (editor), *Conway Letters*, Oxford, 1930.

G. F. Nuttall, *The Holy Spirit in Puritan Faith and Experience*, Oxford, 1947.

C. A. Pierce, *Conscience in the New Testament*, London, 1955.

O. C. Quick, *The Christian Sacraments*, London, 1927.

J. R. Rattenbury, *The Conversion of the Wesleys*, London, 1938.

E. G. Rupp, *Studies in the Making of the English Protestant Tradition*, Cambridge, 1947.

P. Scholes, *The Puritans and Music*, Oxford, 1934.

C. A. Anderson Scott, *Living Issues in the New Testament*, Cambridge, 1933.

R. Seeberg, *History of Christian Doctrines*, (Trans. C. E. Hay), Philadelphia, U.S.A., 1905.

F. J. Shirley, *Richard Hooker and Contemporary Political Ideas*, London, 1949.

J. S. Simon, *John Wesley and the Religious Societies*, London, 1921.

Pearsall Smith (editor), *The Golden Grove*, Oxford, 1930.

C. J. Stranks, *The Life and Writings of Jeremy Taylor*, London, 1952.

N. Sykes, *The Church of England and the Non-Episcopal Churches in the Sixteenth and Seventeenth Centuries*, London, 1948.

 Old Priest and New Presbyter, Cambridge, 1956.

Jeremy Taylor, *Works* (Heber-Eden edition), London, 1861-5.

G. M. Trevelyan, *England under the Stuarts*, London, 1930.

J. Tulloch, *Rational Theology and Christian Philosophy in England in the Seventeenth Century*, 2 vols., Edinburgh, 1874.

G. S. Wakefield, *Puritan Devotion*, London, 1957.

P. S. Watson, *Let God be God!*, London, 1947.

John Wesley, *Journal*, Standard Edition, London, 1909.

 Letters, Standard Edition, 8 vols., London, 1931.

 Works, London, 1841 edition.

H. B. Wheatley, *Diary and Correspondence of John Evelyn*, 3 vols., London, 1906.

H. Ross Williamson, *Jeremy Taylor*, London, 1952.

T. Wood, *English Casuistical Divinity during the Seventeenth Century*, London, 1952.

PAMPHLETS

Baptism Today, London, 1949.

Catholicity, London, 1947.

The Catholicity of Protestantism, London, 1950.

INDEX

181